# The Innovation
# **ANSWER** Book

Teresa Jurgens-Kowal

*Enjoy the Innovation journey!*
*Teresa*

# The Innovation
# **ANSWER** Book

Teresa Jurgens-Kowal
PhD, MBA, PE, NPDP, PMP®, CPEM®

GNPS Press
Houston, Texas USA

ISBN 978-1-70-044995-5

# CONTENTS

# INNOVATION QUESTIONS

# FIGURES

Despite the number of publications, texts, and journals on the topic of innovation, companies still struggle with creating and marketing novel products that meet both customer expectations and profit goals. Innovation is fraught with risk and fails as often as it succeeds. Executives demand better results, yet leaders are unsure what elements in their innovation ecosystem lead to success.

Many books tell great stories of entrepreneurs or mega-corporations that are successful innovators. In *The Innovation ANSWER Book*, we teach YOU how to create a successful innovation ecosystem. This book is accessible to all levels of innovators, new product development practitioners, designers, and developers. Each chapter details persistent innovation questions and presents practical answers that are supported by theory *and* experience.

I've had the wonderful opportunity to consult, coach, and facilitate training workshops in innovation, project management, and creativity with hundreds of different people over the years. I want to express my gratitude to all them for expanding my thinking, giving me feedback on my innovation processes, and for creating enduring professional fellowship. I also want to thank my husband for his patience while I've spent hours and hours distracted by innovation theory to focus on completing this book for you. Luckily, my cats didn't mind my distraction as long as I didn't forget to feed them!

I hope you enjoy *The Innovation ANSWER Book.*


Teresa Jurgens-Kowal
PhD, MBA, PE, NPDP, PMP®, CPEM®, SMC

October 2019

## CHAPTER 1

# INNOVATION FRAMEWORK

*Just as a body, through one, has many parts, but all its many parts form one body... 1 Corinthians 12:12 (NIV)*

## Q1: What is innovation?

A1: Innovation is a process for converting ideas into commercially useful products, services, and programs. Consumers, customers, and end-users purchase products, services, and programs because they bring value and benefit through their use. Innovation includes the introduction of new technologies, unique ways to address market needs, and novel business models. Innovation encompasses activities for new product development (NPD) including research and development (R&D) and integration of service delivery.

## Q2: What is the Innovation Framework?

A2: Frameworks are used in business, engineering, and technical applications to provide guidance and structure to standard work. Serving an essential role, a framework provides a reference for business models and provides a structure for building applications. Using a given framework offers improved quality, repeatability, and saves time in implementation.

The *Flagship Innovation Leader* framework is shown in Figure 1-1 below.

- ***Learning:*** A learning organization is becoming familiar with innovation best practices. Individuals and firms that are starting to learn about innovation best practices may be converting from a start-up venture or solo entrepreneurship into a larger firm. Understanding the fundamentals of new product development

(NPD) and innovation establishes the foundation for long-term success. A learning organization may have some processes in place to manage innovation and is beginning to build teams and leadership skills to tackle more or riskier projects.

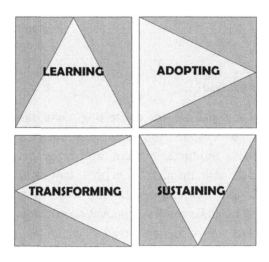

*Figure 1-1: The Flagship Innovation Leader Framework*

- ***Adopting:*** Once a firm has grown beyond one or two successful product launches, the organization searches for processes, policies, and standard work practices to repeat earlier successes. With a growing workforce dedicated to creating new products and in servicing existing product lines, organizations establish standard operating procedures for managing projects and teams to maintain consistent new product delivery to satisfy a growing customer base. Standard NPD processes are implemented across the firm and team members are trained to expand their innovation capabilities.

- ***Transforming:*** As organizations mature in their innovation practices, they transform beyond basic NPD systems to reach top-tier performance in their industry. A firm that transforms its innovation practices into a culture of creativity and collaboration outperforms the competition. Such companies are flexible and institute systems to identify breakthrough ideas and concepts to maintain innovation performance. Innovation work is supported at the highest levels and is recognized as a strategic and competitive advantage.

- **Sustaining:** Any organization that has had success with a new product or service launch cannot rest. Global competition is fierce while both new technologies and new market entrants threaten the status quo. Sustaining a high-performing innovation culture requires leadership dedication to continue learning, adapting, and growing. Innovation leaders benefit from individual coaching and peer group collaborations to transfer emerging best practices for continuous organizational improvement. Sustaining organizations trial and adopt emerging best practices to remain as innovation leaders in their industries.

## Q3: What is the Innovation Health Assessment?

A3: Organizations and individuals benchmark the maturity of their innovation ecosystem through the *Innovation Health Assessment*[1]. The Innovation Health Assessment identifies the stage of innovation maturity (learning, adopting, transforming, or sustaining) through several measures. Gaps in innovation processes are identified, and the health of the innovation system is compared to industry averages. Innovation health is reflected through the following arenas for effective new product and service delivery:

- **Strategic alignment** with business and innovation goals;
- Selective **product portfolio management** to identify and resource the highest-value innovation projects;
- Efficient and simple **new product development (NPD) processes;**

---

[1] Please see the Appendix for more information. Evaluate your company's innovation health at https://simple-pdh.com/courses/innovation-health-assessment/. Instructions for registering for the free assessment are available at https://www.youtube.com/watch?v=-sLGaRaevQ0&t=11s. Please enter code *"Answer Book"* and you will receive a free copy of your *Innovation Health Assessment* report by email.

- Practical product **life cycle management** from idea generation, design and development, commercialization, and retirement;
- Cohesive **teams and leadership** trained in innovation and team processes;
- Customer-focused **market research** with touchpoints built throughout the innovation ecosystem; and
- Functional and transparent **tools and metrics** that support and streamline innovation for the organization.

**Q4:  What does the Innovation Health Assessment look like?**

A4:  An example of the *Innovation Health Assessment* is shown in Figure 1-2 with a sample report included in the Appendix.

*Figure 1-2: Innovation Health Assessment*

The example company data is shown with darker shading and the all-industry average is shown with light shading in Figure 1-2.  An organization with perfect performance in all arenas would have shading to the outer limits of the diagram.  As further discussed in Appendix A, this sample company is in the *Adopting* phase of innovation maturity, compared to an industry average of *Transforming.* Strengths include strategic alignment, managing the product life cycle, gaining customer insights through market research, and implementing supporting tools and metrics. This sample company should focus on building more effective product portfolio management systems and NPD processes as well as training teams and leadership for higher level performance.

**Q5: What are key challenges in innovation today?**

A5: Companies that sustain innovation over the long-term are more successful than their competitors. However, while most CEOs rank innovation as a top priority, they also believe innovation is failing to deliver expected value [1]. Innovation challenges arise with strategic alignment, project selection and execution, and organizational structure. One of the most common failure points for innovation is a lack of upfront research to determine customer needs. However, organizations that follow an integrated system toward innovation maturity have high rates of success.

| INNOVATION TRAPS |
| :--- |
| ➢ Not clarifying the difference between innovation and invention for new product development. |
| ➢ Being unaware of your organization's innovation health and maturity. |
| ➢ Failing to conduct appropriate training for innovation teams and innovation leaders. |
| ➢ Not understanding customer trends and challenges. |

*Instruct the wise and they will be wise still; teach the righteous and they will add to their learning.  Proverbs 9:9 (NIV)*

**Q1:  What are the fundamentals of innovation for a *Learning* organization?**

A1:  A *learning organization* must focus on understanding customer needs and the firm's strategy.  Large numbers of marketers (82%) believe they are innovative, yet only 23% of consumers do [1].  Individuals and firms that are just beginning their innovation journey focus on strategic alignment and customer insights.

## IDENTIFYING INNOVATION STRATEGIES

**Q2:  What is an innovation strategy?**

A2:  Senior management is responsible for developing effective strategies that will profitably grow the business over the long run.  Strategy addresses six key elements [2]:

1.  Deciding what the business is;
2.  Deciding who the customers are and what you have to offer them;
3.  Deciding how you will play the game;
4.  Identifying unique assets and capabilities;
5.  Creating the right organizational environment; and
6.  Identifying and analyzing the impact of trends, competition, and market demand.

### Q3: What is a common innovation strategy for new technology?

A3: One common approach to innovation strategy examines the strength of the firm relative to technology development and market fit [3]. These innovation strategies, known as the Cooper strategies (see Figure 2-1), assume that the firm focuses on only a few key areas for new product development and that the company acts offensively compared to its nearest competitors.

- **Differentiated:** The *differentiated strategy* leads to success with innovation based on new product sales and profitability. Executing this strategy involves deep understanding of customer needs and a highly focused technology development program.
- **High-Budget, Diverse:** Even though firms have large investments in R&D, the *high-budget, diverse strategy* lacks focus for technology development. Moreover, the organization tends to look inward at advancing technical solutions without an understanding of consumer needs.

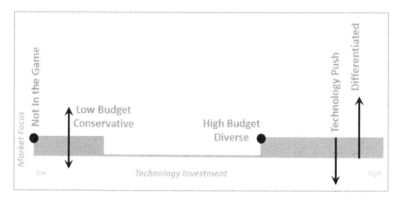

*Figure 2-1: Cooper Strategy Framework*

- **Technology Push:** Like the high-budget, diverse strategy, the *technology push strategy* focuses on internal technical developments. However, in this case, the R&D programs are focused on specific technologies. A drawback of this strategy is a lack of understanding customer needs and the need to develop a market that can absorb the new technology.

- **Conservative:** Many firms invest lightly in R&D and technology development, relying on other parties for major technical breakthroughs. The *conservative strategy* is low risk from the point of view of technology development but results in copycat products that are not highly differentiated from competitors. Market fit is predetermined since the company is developing new products to compete in an established industry.

- **Not-in-the-Game:** Companies undergoing significant change due to mergers or other chaotic business situations often fail to develop a coherent innovation strategy. Innovation is hobbled by a lack of investment in R&D and a lack of understanding of consumer needs.

**Q4: What is an innovation strategy that addresses change?**

A4: Markets, technologies, and consumer tastes can all change rapidly with global competition. Organizations that are risk-seeking adopt innovation strategies that support new technologies launching in new markets. At the opposite end of the spectrum, companies that are risk-averse and have attained a majority market share will resist product development unless their business is threatened. There are four primary innovation strategies that respond to market changes based on the risk tolerance of the organization [4].

- **Prospector:** Companies adopting a *prospector strategy* are risk-seeking and value being first-to-market. With first mover advantages, a firm with a prospector strategy gains most of the early sales in a market but risks losing market share as competition and customers mature.

- **Analyzer:** The *analyzer strategy* balances risk of innovation by accepting product development uncertainties to improve products that have already been introduced into a target market. Companies that follow this strategy focus innovation efforts to support existing product lines to minimize investment.  These firms balance innovation with operational excellence.  Delivering new products to the market that meet customer needs and exceed quality standards helps the analyzer strategy to be successful.

- **Defender:**  Firms that are risk-averse prefer to invest in efficiency of operations rather than new technology developments.  However, if their large market share is threatened by competitors, the company will aggressively develop and market products to maintain their position.  The *defender strategy* results in a resistance to lead radical innovation, but the organization will develop new and innovative features and products to maintain its market position.

- **Reactor:** Companies that undergo significant change, such as mergers and acquisitions or the loss of a founder, struggle to determine a coherent strategy.  Without a specific business or innovation strategy, reactor firms will randomly invest in various innovations without focus on a given technology or target market.  The *reactor strategy* fails over the long-term due to the lack of clearly established innovation goals.

**Q5:  How is the BCG matrix used to analyze strategy?**

A5:  The BCG matrix, originally developed by the Boston Consulting Group in the 1960s, is a visual representation of the products in the company's portfolio and includes competition to evaluate the balance of an innovation strategy.  As indicated in Figure 2-2, the BCG matrix illustrates market share on the x-axis and market growth on the y-axis. Traditionally, the horizontal axis for market share is shown decreasing from a high level on the left side to a low level on the right side of the graph.  By plotting the number or type of products in each quadrant, management can discern organizational strengths and competitive threats.  This analysis drives innovation strategy as well as selection of active NPD projects.

- **Stars:** Products that have high market share and generate significant revenue are considered *stars*. First-to-market products often are termed stars but will convert to cash cows as more competitors enter the market. New and existing products that fall into the stars category are good investments yet often require continued cash influx due to the high growth rates.

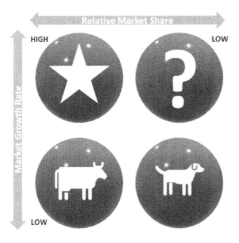

*Figure 2-2: BCG Matrix*

- **Cash Cows:** Products in the cash cow category of the BCG matrix are ones in which the firm has a high category market share or brand recognition. Yet, the overall growth in the market is slowing. These products generate profits since the expenses to maintain them are low while revenues are high. Organizations should monitor cash cows in case competition or technology changes occur that would transition these products into dogs.
- **Dogs:** Products at the end of their life cycle are frequently termed *dogs*. They have both a low market share and a low growth rate. Revenues and expenses are nearly equal, yet the organization has some burden to maintain these products in the portfolio and to support sales and marketing. Senior

management must decide whether to retire these products, divest the product line, or rejuvenate the product through NPD investment for a next generation product.

- **Question Marks:** Existing or new products that are new to a market and involve new technologies are often considered *question marks*. These products have a potentially high growth rate but have a small market share requiring large investments of financial and human resources. When the product is a new-to-the-world offering, it has the potential to transition to a star. Investment decisions are made based on the potential for growth and aggressiveness of competition in the market.

**Q6: What is a business model?**

A6: Strategy describes the mission, vision, and values of a firms, laying out the purpose of the organization. A *business model* is more specific in that is describes how an organization can create and capture value as well as how customers, vendors, and distributors share in value capture. The *business model canvas* is a simple and effective strategy tool for organizations of all sizes. Business models address four main areas of a business: customers, the offer, infrastructure, and financial viability.

**Q7: What is the business model canvas?**

A7: As a visual tool, the *business model canvas* is intended to be displayed on a single sheet of paper [5]. Elements on the right (see Figure 2-3) focus on the customer, while elements on the left are driven by the business. Customer focus areas include segments (1) and relationships (2) as well as channels (3) and revenue streams (4) for the business. Business elements include partners (5), resources (6), activities (7), and costs (8). Note that the value proposition (9) is at the center of the business model canvas since it overlaps and links customers and the business. A brief description of each element follows.

1. **Customer Segments**: Organizations focus on a broad range of customers that are divided into distinctive customer segments with their own specific needs and requirements. This allows tailoring of the value proposition, customer relationships, and channels for each segment. Successful businesses make clear choices regarding which segments to serve and which to ignore.

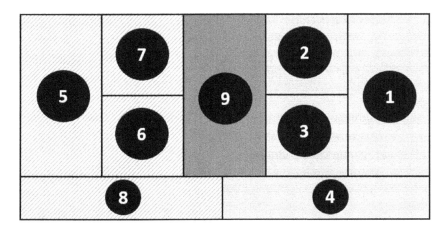

*Figure 2-3: Example of Business Model Canvas*

2. **Customer Relationships**: This section of the business model canvas addresses which type of relationship is required for each customer segment. Customer relationships range from automated interactions to very personal, high-touch relationships. In describing the firm's strategic approach to customer relationships, the business addresses delivery of the customer experience, associated costs, and maintenance of customer interactions.

3. **Channels:** Within the business model canvas, channels describe how the product will reach the customer (distribution), and how the customer will learn about products (communication), and how customers will purchase products and services (sales). The company may directly control sales

and distribution channels, or it may partner with others to indirectly reach customer segments through retail stores or websites.

4. **Revenue:** Of course, a strategy is only valuable to a firm if it produces profitable outcomes. Revenue is the cash generated when a company sells its goods and services. A variety of revenue models are used by firms, and a company must select appropriate revenue streams to demonstrate how and when customers will pay.

5. **Key Partners:** Partners are the external companies and suppliers necessary for the business to perform key activities and deliver value to its customers. Buyer-seller relationships optimize operations and reduce risk associated with the business. Partnerships also include alliances with non-competitors, joint ventures that reduce risk, improved customer relationships, and external opportunities to increase revenues and reduce costs.

6. **Key Resources:** Resources include time, money, equipment, and talent. Key resources are the most important strategic assets for a firm and are not easily acquired or imitated by competitors. Physical resources include assets such as plant, equipment, manufacturing facilities, access to raw materials, and inventory. Talent, or intellectual resources, include proprietary knowledge, brands, patents, and licensing agreements.

7. **Key Activities:** An organization's strategy is supported by key activities, processes, and policies. Such activities allow the organization to operate effectively and address how the customer value proposition is supported. These activities may include novel distribution channels, unique customer relationships, and special networks or platforms. Competitors have difficulty to mimic the key activities of a successful business, yielding an advantage to the organization.

8. **Cost Structure:** Cost is the counterpart to revenue since revenue less cost is profit. Two primary cost models are cost-

driven and value-driven. *Cost-driven organizations* seek to minimize all costs, while *value-driven companies* focus more on delivering customer value in terms of quality or prestige. Many companies establish a cost structure between these two extremes. The firm's strategy is reflected by the cost structure.

9. **Value Proposition:** Perhaps the most important element of the business model canvas is the *value proposition*. The value proposition describes a bundle of products, services, applications, and programs that the company delivers to the customer segment(s) of interest. It describes why these customers value a particular solution based on their problem statement. In designing a strategy, firms address which customer problems it is solving, how customer needs are satisfied, and why the customer values a given product or service experience. The value proposition defines how an organization differentiates itself from competition by focusing on price, service, speed-to-market, and delivery for the customer. The value proposition also defines quality of design, brand status, customer experience, and overall satisfaction.

**Q8:  What is a sustainability strategy for innovation?**

A8:  Sustainability addresses the *triple bottom line* of planet, people, and profit (see Figure 2-4). Many organizations today publish formal sustainability strategies and use the concept of the triple bottom line as a driver for innovation and product development. Sustainable innovation is a multi-disciplinary activity going beyond regulatory compliance. For example, new product development projects selected within the active project portfolio often score high on sustainability metrics such as reduction in emissions or reduced waste [6].

Measuring the success of a sustainability strategy is a long-term endeavor. Functional departments and senior management create sustainable innovations and integrate both suppliers and customers in product development. Investment in sustainable innovation requires developing and leveraging capabilities throughout the product life cycle. Tools for sustainable innovation include many design mechanisms, known collectively as "D4X".

In the triple bottom line, *planet* generally refers to protecting the environment and minimizing the impact of current generations to preserve conditions for future generations. *People* refers to the labor force as well as the communities in areas that are used for resource and raw material generation. Fair wages, appropriate living conditions, and opportunities for future benefit factor into this element of the triple bottom line. Finally, *profit* is necessary so that organizations can invest in under-privileged areas of the world, provide living wage employment, and fund environmental clean-up activities. All three components work together and are considered part of a sustainable innovation strategy.

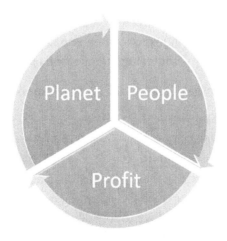

*Figure 2-4: Triple Bottom Line of Sustainability*

### Q9: What does D4X mean?

A9: D4X is an abbreviation used throughout the new product development life cycle to focus the innovation effort on specific parameters, such as design for environment (D4E), design for maintenance (D4M), design for reusability (D4R), design for service (D4S), or design for disposal (D4D) [7].

For instance, D4E includes sustainability measures to minimize the risks a product imparts on the environment from the sourcing of raw materials to manufacture, use, and end-of-life. Likewise, D4R builds robustness into the product design so that if a part or piece of the product fails, it is not necessary to discard the entire product. This benefits the manufacturer, the user, and the environment by diverting usable parts from the waste stream and reusing them to create other pieces. Finally, D4D is often overlooked. Disposal involves consideration during the development process of the product itself but also the packaging materials to minimize waste streams.

## GATHERING CUSTOMER INSIGHTS

**Q10: What is the leading cause of failure for new products?**

A10: The leading cause of failure for new products is a lack of upfront homework by the developer and a mismatch of marketing with target customers. Innovation is successful when customer needs are determined prior to R&D, technology development, and product design. Tools and techniques, like market research and Design Thinking, provide methodologies to understand customer needs and to build these insights into the product development process.

**Q11: What is market research?**

A11: *Market research* is a study of customer wants and needs, gathering and analyzing information about what consumers like and expect, and understanding how and why customers make specific purchases. Traditional market research utilizes *secondary* and *primary* techniques that provide both *qualitative* and *quantitative* data.

Some market research methods explore and discover customer needs, while other types of market research gather customer data and product use information. Poor decisions in market research become more costly and the risk of bad data influencing commercial decisions increases as a new product advances toward final launch. Thus, the type and category of market research are linked to the various stages of product development and what customer requirements need to be addressed.

**Q12:  What questions should market research answer?**

A12:    Information that is sought by market research during an innovation project includes the following decisions.

- What opportunities are available currently?
- What future opportunities are available?
- What do customers need?
- Are customer needs clearly articulated, or are they unstated?
- What are the drivers for customers to purchase products?
- What motivates a customer to repurchase products?
- How is the value proposition described for the brand or product?
- How can the product be refined to become more attractive or desirable to the target customer audience?
- Will customers buy the product and how often?
- Is the product a one-time purchase or a subscription?
- What is the price point and pricing strategy for the product?
- Where do customers find the product and where do they purchase it?
- Are there accessories or complementary products for sale with the product?
- Are there competitive product solutions available in the marketplace?
- Who are competitors, direct and indirect?
- What differentiates the new product from other products?
- Is the product sustainable?

**Q13:  What is secondary market research?**

A13: *Secondary market research* is normally conducted before primary market research because it is less expensive and lays the groundwork for future studies.  Gathering and analyzing already published data helps an innovation team validate customer needs as well as to scope the degree of competition in the marketplace. Additionally, secondary market research provides the context and constraints for further market studies (primary research).

A key advantage of secondary market research is that it is inexpensive since the data is already available. Cautions for using secondary market research abound, however. The innovation team must understand why and how the data was collected and whether it is relevant to the product development effort they are considering. Secondary market research can be either qualitative or quantitative in nature.

**Q14: What is primary market research?**

A14: *Primary market research* is an original study of consumer behaviors or tastes that is conducted fully within the control of the organization. Because specific questions are addressed with primary market research, it can be expensive. A key outcome of primary market research yields unique information for target product features and attributes as well as how customers think and feel about the innovation. Primary market research can be qualitative or quantitative.

**Q15: What is qualitative market research?**

A15: Firms use *qualitative market research* to gather initial customer needs and to gauge the reactions of potential customer to an idea or concept. Qualitative market research gathers stories, opinions, and anecdotes from potential consumers to understand emotional and behavioral needs for an innovation.

Normally, qualitative market research involves a small sample size since the techniques for gathering data are labor-intensive, involving direct customer observation and interviewing. The purpose of qualitative market research is to gain understanding of what problems a customer faces and why they might select a given product solution.

## Q16:  What does voice of customer mean?

A16:  *Voice of customer (VOC)* is a market research term applied to a variety of techniques that capture customer requirements and feedback.  VOC includes structured, in-depth interviews to determine customer needs.  It is a primary market research method, typically involving small numbers of potential customers and focuses on gathering their impressions of needs and feedback regarding product concepts or prototypes.  The customer perspective is invaluable to successfully identifying product features.

## Q17:  What is quantitative market research?

A17:  Unlike qualitative market research that identifies subjective customer needs, *quantitative market research* classifies and categorizes consumer and product information with statistical data. Quantitative market research data benefits an innovation team during business case development and the latter stages of an innovation project to validate customer need, market size, sales volume, and product pricing.

Just as secondary market research frames the context for primary market research, much of the information determined in qualitative studies sets the stage for detailed quantitative research.  Most traditional market research tools are classified as either qualitative or quantitative, though there may be overlap between techniques used in secondary and primary market research.  Much of the quantitative data used by an innovation team for decision-making is secondary.

Sources of secondary market research include quantitative data published by governments, trade magazines, scientific journals, white papers, online information, and open source databases.  Secondary market research has the advantage of being low cost and requiring a short time to collect from a wide variety of sources often with access to the full database.  However, innovation teams using such data are cautioned to examine the information for accuracy, reliability, and recency. Quantitative market research from public data sources is valuable to gain information on market and technology trends.

**Q18: What are other ways to categorize market research?**

A18: The terms *exploratory market research* and *confirmatory market research* are sometimes used in product development. Exploratory market research is often used in the early stages of a project to identify customer needs and to determine if potential concepts are a fit for the market. Like qualitative market research, exploratory studies gather observations and stories about customer problems. The sample size is typically small for exploratory research but may involve a broad scope.

Confirmatory market research, on the other hand, is used to validate ideas, concepts, and product design features. It may be either qualitative or quantitative but is focused on testing a specific hypothesis regarding the innovation to validate assumptions, specifications, and other design criteria. Sample sizes vary with the type of confirmatory research tool deployed but the scope of the study is usually narrow.

**Q19: What are the steps in market research?**

A19: There are six steps in the market research process, as shown in Figure 2-5.

*Figure 2-5: Steps in Market Research*

- **Define the problem.** *Defining the problem* includes fashioning a clear statement of what data and information is sought and what questions the market research project is seeking to address.

- **Define the accuracy required for results.** Accuracy in quantitative market research describes the acceptable level of statistical confidence and experimental error. Higher accuracy is needed during later innovation stages, especially for making critical go-to-market decisions.
- **Collect the data.** A suitable methodology is selected and applied to collect appropriate information that addresses the problem with the required level of accuracy.
- **Analyze the data and interpret the information.** An appropriate analysis technique is applied to provide a summary of results that addresses the specific problem. Many different statistical analysis tools and methods are available, including regression, cluster analysis, and multi-variate procedures. Information is assembled in a format to draw conclusions from the market research data.
- **Draw a conclusion.** Results of the market research study are interpreted to draw specific, actionable conclusions regarding the innovation project based on inputs from potential customers.
- **Implement the action.** Findings from market research are applied to the specific problem and influence decisions to continue advancing the product development effort. Alternatively, a lack of customer engagement can lead to discontinuing the project.

**Q20: What are some tools used in secondary market research?**

A20: The purpose of secondary market research is to identify market opportunities and to begin segmenting the market for focusing the product development effort. Innovation teams gather information regarding customer problems, how these problems are addressed with current product solutions, and customer satisfaction with competitive products. As indicated earlier, sources of secondary market information include simple internet searches, trade publications, government statistics, reports from consultancies, and white papers. Internal company data provides additional context to frame product development projects. Social media information is also used to gain an understanding of customer issues and potential end-users' attitudes and feelings toward existing product solutions.

**Q21:  What are some techniques used in primary market research?**

A21:   There are a wide variety of tools and techniques that help determine fit and focus for a product concept and to validate the product design.

- **Customer Site Visits:**  A *customer site visit* is a qualitative market research technique in which members of the innovation team visit potential customers at their site. Important elements of a customer site visit include that the potential customer is vested in the identified problem, is open to sharing opinions and use cases, and offers open access to the innovation team for observation.  Having both end-users and decision-makers from the customer organization available during the site visit increases the quality of data gathered.

- **Surveys:** *Surveys* vary from simple to highly sophisticated and can be administered in many ways.  Exploratory research uses a survey format that is interactive, much like a customer interview.  Data from closed-end surveys (with predetermined questions and answers) is statistically significant for large samples.   Surveys with additional open-ended questions combine quantitative and qualitative data so that the innovation team can link motivation with specific responses. Distribution methods range from internet and email delivery, direct mail, and in-person or telephone surveys.  Response rates greater than 20% are excellent; therefore, a large volume of surveys is typically distributed to gather statistically significant data for analysis.

- **Concept Testing:**   During the early stages of product development, new concepts are tested to determine whether there is a market for the product or service.  In a *concept test*, a narrative description, image, or prototype of the product is presented to a target customer. Potential customers indicate their understanding of the product concept, discuss whether the product features offer expected benefits, and provide initial purchase intentions. Data gathered from concept tests are qualitative and used to refine the product design throughout the product development process. A key outcome of concept testing is to eliminate poor concepts and weak ideas.

- **Sensory Testing:** Generally, *sensory testing* is considered a quantitative market research technique that evaluates products by measuring human sensory responses (such as sight, hearing, smell, touch, or taste). Sensory testing is used extensively for consumer products and to explore concepts in early phases as well as to validate product performance prior to launch. *Eye tracking*, for example, follows human subjects by measuring where people look and for how long. Results include a visual scan that overlays the image of the object being tested. It is used to address questions regarding customer reactions to various stimuli, especially in an online environment.

- **Focus Groups:** A *focus group* is a group interview technique led by a trained moderator that uses collaboration as a primary communication tool. Focus group participants are usually screened to indicate a match with the target market segment and involve six to ten people in each group discussion. Often, focus groups are held in specialized facilities so that the innovation team can observe the study and interactions of potential customers. Recordings and transcripts of the focus group provide feature data and information for evaluation. The primary goal of a focus group is to learn how potential customers think and feel about a product or proposed product solution, including interacting with prototypes during the session. A key benefit of focus groups is the collaboration among participants.

- **Product Use Testing:** In the later stages of product development, the innovation team seeks to understand how well the product features and design meet the needs of customers. In an *alpha test*, a pre-production model of the product is tested internally. This allows the innovation team to make any last-minute quality or manufacturing adjustments for the new product. *Beta tests* are generally used in the software and IT fields to test pre-production products in live environments. Results of a beta test include how the product interacts with other systems. Finally, a *gamma test* is used to test a product to verify that customers are satisfied. Gamma tests are frequently deployed in the pharmaceutical and medical device industries to ensure that the product addresses the end-user's problem but does not introduce significant or unpleasant side effects that would prevent widespread adoption of the product.
- **Market Testing:** As a product nears commercial launch, the marketing plan and collateral are tested simultaneously with the final product design in market testing. Market tests vary from a *full rollout* of advertising and brand campaigns to faux product sales in which the marketing materials are presented to the customer, but the product is not transferred. A hybrid case of market testing is a *controlled sale* where the ordering and distribution systems are bypassed but the customer is exposed to the full marketing materials and receives the product for use.
- **Conjoint Analysis:** *Conjoint analysis* is a statistical technique that measures the value potential customers place on different attributes of the new product or service. Several different features are presented to potential consumers at varying levels so that the product development team determines the best combination of features. With sufficient input data, conjoint analysis produces statistically significant results as a primary market research technique.

## Q22: What is ethnographic market research?

A22: *Ethnography* is the study of customers or end-users in relation to their environment. Market researchers use field observations to gain a deeper understanding of customers, their lifestyles, culture, and interactions to uncover unarticulated needs. *Ethnographic market research* uses a variety of techniques to generate a complete vision of customers and how they use products and services in their daily lives.

Typically, ethnographic market research occurs at the site of the customers' use of the product or service, such as the place or location where the product is used or at their home. This allows observation and inquiry to provide further insight for the product development effort. Immersion studies are used to observe larger markets, especially for geographical expansion of product lines into new places.

Gaining direct interaction and feedback from customers is the primary advantage of ethnographic market research. It is a useful technique to uncover unarticulated needs and can serve as the basis for radical new product development. NPD teams are cautioned, however, that ethnographic research can be time-consuming in order to collect a broad sample of the target market(s). Ethnographic research yields qualitative results.

## Q23: What is human-centered design?

A23: *Human-centered design* is an approach to innovation and customer insights that considers the user or customer at the center of the design process. A core assumption is that people themselves hold the answers to their needs and desires. Market research and product development follow three phases in human-centered design: inspiration, ideation, and implementation. The process is iterative, moving from concrete customer observations to abstract concepts and then back to concrete ones.

As a broad category of Design Thinking, human-centered design focuses on building empathy for customers, creating ideas, generating prototypes, and testing potential product solutions with customers.

Feedback from customers is critical to success of the process. Human-centered design involves intimate market research to observe people and their problems in their own environment and yields effective product solutions that are built on empathetic customer insights.

**Q24:  How is social media used for market research?**

A24:  Nearly all companies in developed countries use some form of social media to conduct exploratory market research. Social media "listening" is used for co-creation and in the early design stages. Innovation teams also use social media to test and compare marketing programs for product launch; sometimes, new products are launched exclusively via social media platforms.

A caution in using social media in market research is that the information can be biased and may not reach all participants in a given market. On the other hand, if the market for a new product is defined narrowly, social media can target the specific outlets for a customer segment and yield excellent qualitative data.

Social media market research has the advantage of providing direct and immediate contact with both existing and potential customers. Further, social media allow a firm to engage with lead users and product evangelists for ongoing idea generation and input throughout the product design process.

## CONTEMPORARY INNOVATION MODELS

**Q25:  What is disruptive innovation?**

A25:  Clayton Christensen broke ground with his 1997 book, *"The Innovator's Dilemma,"* in which he describes the challenges that incumbent organizations have in developing competitive new business models [8]. *Disruptive innovations* involve new technologies or novel business models that create products or services whose application changes an industry substantially, shifting competition and consumer tastes.

One framework of disruption involves a producer deploying new technology to compete with existing products in which the new technology is inferior to a standard performance measure of the competitive products, but it offers a new convenience. For example, e-readers initially had quality issues in presenting text but offered the convenience of a small storage space for multiple books. Often the disruptive innovation is launched by a firm that is much smaller than the existing competition. Such start-ups are willing to accept lower end markets and lesser profits while bigger, incumbent companies require large volume, high-margin sales to compete.

Another model of disruptive innovation involves simplified products introduced into markets where customers were previously not served by large, incumbent companies. For instance, mobile banking applications in nations with developing economies give consumers access to savings and loan accounts without needing to visit bank branches. Many of these new banking customers previously had no access to financial services due to living in remote locations or lacked traditional deposit requirements.

**Q26: What does "Jobs-to-Be-Done" mean?**

A26: Foundational in Christensen's disruptive innovation theory [8] is the concept of "jobs-to-be-done." Customers seek solutions to jobs that they need to do rather than wanting products or features. Disruptive innovations can address the job-to-be-done with simple, uncomplicated products or with new technologies that offer convenience to the consumer. Innovators need to understand what challenges, or jobs-to-be-done, that customers face from an emotional and behavioral standpoint. Understanding these tasks and the desire of customers to solve the problem helps determine consumer motivation leading to better new product designs.

**Q27: What is open innovation?**

A27: *Open innovation* complements the theory of disruptive innovation. The term open innovation was coined by Henry

Chesbrough [9] in 2003 and acknowledges that ideas are generated both inside and outside the walls of a corporation. Traditional, or "closed innovation", used internal R&D to create product improvements within an organization that served existing customers. Such companies were highly integrated from the sources of fundamental research, raw materials acquisition, manufacturing, marketing, sales, and service. In contrast, open innovation capitalizes on external sources of ideas and outside partners to take a product to market.

Open innovation takes many forms. In generating ideas, companies use universities to conduct research, invest in technology through start-ups, and license know-how from suppliers, vendors, and even competitors. When firms generate knowledge that is not aligned with their strategic goals, they may license the technology to a partner that is better positioned to utilize it.

### Q28: How is intellectual property protected in open innovation?

A28: *Intellectual property (IP)* represents the patents, trademarks, copyrights, brands, and trade secrets of a firm. Large corporations may hesitate to use open innovation for fear of losing control of their intellectual property. However, organizations benefit financially by sharing their inventions through licensing agreements and shared revenue models with alliance partners. Society and markets, in general, benefit from greater deployment of technology inventions including those released through open innovation models.

### Q29: What is a product roadmap?

A29: Product roadmaps are visual depictions showing the path from the current state to future product releases. Significant milestones include new feature and next generation product launches. Product roadmaps link business and marketing strategies and are shared publicly with both customers and vendors. The product roadmap helps the organization to plan investment and marketing campaigns around significant product events.

Roadmaps are especially useful for planning new platform products and the derivative products associated with them. For example, automobiles have a standard platform of engine, chassis, and transmission that is updated less frequently (e.g. every seven to ten years) than the annual release of new car models. A product roadmap shows the pathway from today's engine, chassis, transmission, and styling to a future car with new engine, chassis, and transmission with intermittent year styling updates.

**Q30: What is a technology roadmap?**

A30: A technology roadmap complements the product roadmap but is used primarily for internal strategic planning. Technology for innovation is developed in-house and is acquired from external sources. The technology roadmap provides a visual display of what, when, where, and how technical resources and R&D achievements are required during a given time frame to design and develop new products and features. Technology advancements often cross functional lines and the technology roadmap indicates internal and external knowledge transfer to accelerate innovation.

In many cases, a strategic marketing plan works backward from the desired future state and product vision, marking significant technical deliverables required to launch a new product on a specific date. Roadmaps are guides to implementing the strategy and ensuring that customer trends are incorporated into the technical design as well as the overall product development effort.

## DESIGN THINKING
**Q31: What is Design Thinking?**

A31: *Design Thinking (DT)* is a creative and collaborative problem-solving methodology that focuses on customer empathy to generate practical solutions. DT is an iterative process as illustrated in Figure 2-6. At a high level, the first step in DT is to identify a problem and the second step is to solve the problem. In identifying a problem, however, an innovation team must *discover* customer needs many of which are unarticulated. Next, these needs must be *defined* as a clear and concise problem statement that is aligned with the organization's strategic innovation goals.

Once the problem statement is defined, the innovation team uses divergent thinking to *create* as many possible solutions alternatives as they can. With many ideas available to test, an optimum solution to the customer's problem is generated.

Testing of potential product solutions is the last step in the iterative DT model. Rapid prototyping and fast failure are used to *evaluate* features, attributes, and product solutions. Feedback from customers (discover) drives further refinement of the problem statement (define), allowing the team to generate additional concepts for the product solution (create), and testing of these ideas (evaluate) until the final product solution is devised.

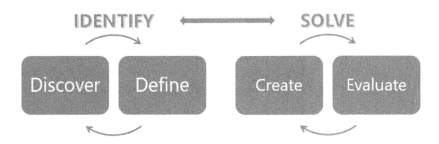

*Figure 2-6: Design Thinking Model*

**Q32: What are some *discovery tools* in DT?**

A32: There are several tools used in Design Thinking to uncover customer needs, especially those that are difficult for a consumer to explain (unarticulated needs). Discovery tools include the following.

- **Observation:** DT is built on customer empathy – understanding not only what the customer needs but also why. *Observation* is a great way to understand what problems a customer faces, how they currently address these issues, and what they experience as they use current product solutions. The innovation team will ask qualitative questions during observation to gather information on how a customer chooses a product solution, why they chose the one they did, and how they feel about using the existing products. Observation is a form of ethnographic market research.

- **Interviews:** Like observation, *customer interviews* seek to learn how customers think and feel about the problems they face and the existing product solutions for those problems. Interviews span from informal inquiry of customers in a retail setting to structured question-and-response sessions, such as in a focus group. Interviews are used in business-to-consumer (B2C) situations while *site visits* are used for business-to-business (B2B). The methodology is generally the same with the major difference in terminology.

- **Journaling:** An innovation team can generate a lot of empathy for customers by following their daily activities in a *journal*. The product development team will select a segment of existing customers and potential customers, and ask them to capture their thoughts, feelings, experiences, and interactions in a journal. People can use whatever form of journaling is relevant to them, so that the innovation team may review text narratives, images, sketches, and so on to gather deep understanding of how customers feel about themselves and their relationships with other people, products, and services.

**Q33: What are some tools used for *defining the problem* in DT?**

A33: The goal of the Define stage in DT is to ensure that the innovation team has correctly identified the customer's problem and that the problem statement is clear and concise. Note that many DT tools can be used in multiple stages of the process since understanding customer empathy is a key objective for successful innovation. A few tools used for defining the problem in DT follow.

- **Customer Empathy Map:** The vast majority of product purchase decisions is emotional. A *customer empathy map* helps the team understand the emotional aspects of the problem and can lead to deeper insights in solving the problem. Sub-teams of three or four people view the problem through the eyes of one customer such that all customer segments are represented by the full innovation team. The goal is to document what the customer thinks and feels, what they see and hear, and what they say and do. Additionally, the team will record obstacles ("pains") the customer faces in solving the problem and benefits ("gains") expected from solving the problem. A sample customer empathy map is shown in Figure 2-7 with suggested queries for the team to define the problem from the customer's perspective.

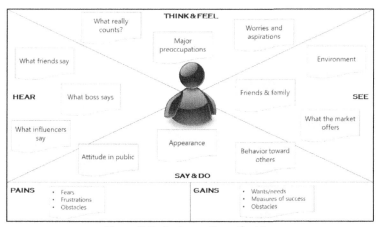

*Figure 2-7: Customer Empathy Map*

- **Customer Journey Map:** Sometimes known as a *customer experience map*, the *customer journey map* traces the customer's interaction throughout the product purchase-use-disposal cycle. This includes each step customers take once they become aware of their problem, researching options for solving the problem, how they make a choice, and how they make a purchase. Of course, the customer's interaction with a product is not complete without documenting after-sales support and disposal, recycle, or replacement of the product. Typically, several different personas representing different market segments, are traced on the same customer journey map. Elements in the decision-making process that are challenges for customers are indicated so that the innovation team can further discover and define these problems.

- **5 Whys:** The technique of "5 Whys" has its origin in the world of Six Sigma and quality management. In order to understand the root cause of a problem, an innovation team member will probe a potential customer by asking "Why?" several times. A simple example follows showing that the root cause of the problem requires in-depth probing.
  - *Why are you late for work?* My car stopped.
  - *Why did your car stop?* It ran out of gas.
  - *Why did you run out of gas?* I didn't fill the tank today.
  - *Why did you not fill the gas tank?* I didn't have any money.
  - *Why do you not have money?* I forgot to cash my paycheck.

The solution to the problem of being late for work is not obvious. A potential answer might be direct deposit so that the employee's money is immediately available on payday.

## Q34: What are some methods used in the *create* stage of DT?

A34: Many different tools are useful in the Create stage of DT. Most of these tools capitalize on divergent thinking to generate as many ideas as possible that might address the customer's problem as defined by the innovation team. Ideation tools for divergent thinking are varied and the team will select techniques that are best suited for the scale of the problem and the scope of the stakeholders involved. Generating ideas for features, functions, and applications should involve the customer, the innovation team, cross-functional company representatives, suppliers and distributors, people from adjacent industries, and other creative personalities. Some typical tools used for divergent thinking include the following.

- **Brainwriting:** Most people are familiar with *brainstorming*, an ideation technique used to generate a lot of ideas in a short period of time. *Brainwriting* [10] is a slight modification of the brainstorming technique that typically generates more and better ideas. In brainstorming, a question is posed to a group and individuals will verbally call out ideas that are subsequently recorded for the group to review later. A disadvantage of brainstorming is that the ideas of more reserved group members can be overlooked and there are few opportunities to redirect the group from emerging themes or concepts.

  Brainwriting, on the other hand, involves posing the problem to the group before the session. During the ideation session, individuals will write down specific ideas they have to address the problem. After a short amount of time passes (about 30 seconds), everyone passes their sheet of paper to another person in the group. The second person can add a new idea or build from the idea already recorded. Again, after a short amount of time passes, everyone passes their paper to another person in the group, and the process repeats.

  After a few cycles of recording new ideas and building on previous concepts, the paper is returned to the person who recorded the first idea. Each group member selects the best idea from the list that was just generated and shares that with the group. Collaboration and communication are enhanced in brainwriting and it is a more successful ideation tool than brainstorming.

- **SCAMPER:** The acronym SCAMPER is used to trigger alternate associations of existing product solutions and different perspectives of customers and stakeholders in addressing the problem statement.
    - ○ **Substitute:** Can you exchange product parts or raw materials to generate a new product solution? Can you use a product from another market?

- o **Combine:** Can you add different elements together to come up with a new product concept? What is the outcome of combining different products to achieve multiple goals with one product instead?
- o **Adapt:** How can we adjust the existing products or processes to improve them? What else can be done to yield better results?
- o **Modify:** What if we had twice the number of customers? What would the product look like if we used half the raw materials?
- o **Put to Another Use:** Which components of the product can be used in other products? Can we replace any aspect of the product or service package with something else?
- o **Eliminate:** What happens if we remove components of the product? How can we achieve the same output if we eliminate steps in the process?
- o **Reverse:** What if we do the process backwards? Can we switch the order that components are considered in the product or service application?

- **TRIZ:** Developed by GS Altshuler, TRIZ is the Russian acronym for the *Theory of Inventive Problems Solving* (also known by the English acronym TIPS). *TRIZ* is a methodology based on logic that accelerates a team's creative capacity. It provides structure in generating ideas to solve problems by examining patterns of typical problems and solutions. As shown in Figure 2-8, the TRIZ methodology consists of learning repeating patterns of problem-solution pairs. An innovation team translates the specific problem to a generalized problem and then determines the general solution. This generalized solution is then translated to a specific solution for the problem at hand. Typically, teams trained in the TRIZ methodology for creative problem-solving consider 40 different principles at the root of every general problem-solution pair. These principles include concepts such as symmetry, merging, and segmentation of products and features.

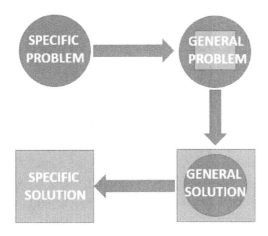

*Figure 2-8: TRIZ Model of Creative Problem-Solving*

**Q35: What are some typical tools and techniques for evaluating ideas in DT?**

A35: During the *Solve* stage of Design Thinking, the innovation team is considering which aspects of potential solutions will address the customer's needs and leave them satisfied. Many of the tools deployed in the *create* stage result in long lists of ideas that must be translated into actionable and tangible product features. While ideation tools involve divergent thinking, the large number of ideas are categorized into themes or generalized areas of design and development in convergent thinking. Convergent thinking harmonizes ideas and concepts from divergent thinking in the prior step. Three common tools and techniques for evaluating ideas in the Design Thinking model are affinity diagrams, SWOT analysis, and rapid prototyping.

- **Affinity Diagrams:** One tool for organizing the information generated during ideation is an *affinity diagram*. An affinity diagram is usually created by the same team that participated in the divergent thinking portion of the ideation session. All ideas are recorded on sticky notes and similar ideas are grouped together. The innovation team, including customer representatives as appropriate, continue to study and analyze groupings of ideas until three to five categories or themes are clearly identified to move forward in the process. These are typically actionable and concrete concepts, such as those that will be tested with rapid prototyping.

- **SWOT Analysis:** SWOT is an acronym for *strengths, weaknesses, opportunities,* and *threats.* Customer challenges, product ideas, and feature concepts are categorized according to internal and external factors (see Figure 2-9). A company takes advantage of new product ideas for which they have internal strengths and capabilities and are ideas that demonstrate large market opportunities. On the other hand, product features and attributes for which the company has little experience are considered weaknesses. The firm will make strategic decisions whether to develop these capabilities, acquire technology from outside the firm, or to abandon the concept. Likewise, the company evaluates threats to the market from external competitors, including regulations, environment, and legislation to determine a path forward for the idea or concept.

*Figure 2-9: SWOT Analysis Framework*

In Design Thinking, there is a bias toward making and testing products and features to gain customer inputs. Rapid prototyping includes testing parts or pieces of the final product quickly to evaluate customer satisfaction. Standalone design elements are tested to determine functionality without having to build and integrate a complete product. The goal of rapid prototyping is to gain knowledge of the technology as well as user interactions and customer satisfaction. Fast failure is an outcome of rapid prototyping. Innovation teams learn quickly from what does not work and incorporate that knowledge into the next iteration of design and development.

**INNOVATION TRAPS FOR A LEARNING ORGANIZATION**

➤ Not creating and communicating a clear, concise innovation strategy across all organizational levels.
➤ Not doing your upfront market research to fully understand customer needs.
➤ Doing expensive primary market research without first screening with secondary market research.
➤ Designing sustaining innovations to support existing markets only and risking disruption by a competitor.
➤ Limiting actionable insights from direct customer interactions by not taking advantage of open innovation and Design Thinking.

*Stand firm, and you will win life.  Luke 21:19 (NIV)*

**Q1:   What are the fundamentals of innovation for an *Adopting* organization?**

A1:   An *adopting organization* is one that has built fundamental understanding of why innovation is important to long-term success and is beginning to formalize processes and policies to support growth in innovation.   But, understanding and implementing a repeatable process for innovation and new product development require unique skills and practices.   Adopting organizations begin to standardize product development processes and design project management processes for innovation that yield repeatable and predictable outcomes.  Forming the appropriate team structure for each project, depending on the complexity and risk, help firms allocate scarce resources while capitalizing on the most value-added projects.

## TYPES OF INNOVATION PROCESSES

**Q2: What is an NPD process?**

A2:   A typical new product development (NPD) process is one that follows a series of stages with the aim of decreasing risk as investment in the product development effort increases.   Traditional NPD processes include phases to identify market and technology opportunities, concept generation, product design selection, evaluation and testing, production, and launch [1].  There are several commonly implemented innovation processes based upon the culture of the organization, risk tolerance of stakeholders, and the pace of change in the markets and technologies of key industries.  Some of these are illustrated in Figure 3-1.

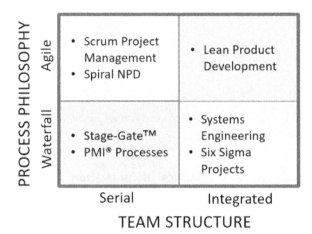

*Figure 3-1: Innovation Processes*

*WATERFALL PROJECT MANAGEMENT PHILOSOPHY*
## Q3: What is a waterfall process?

A3: Many traditional project management processes are described as "waterfall" processes since each stage of work must be completed before the next stage can start. This is much like the flow of water from a waterfall cascading from one level to the next. A key feature of waterfall project management processes is that project planning is quite extensive and is completed prior to any project work being initiated. Waterfall projects may involve hand-offs of work between teams for large efforts or may integrate multi-disciplinary teams throughout the project life cycle. As shown in Figure 3-1, waterfall processes with serial teamwork assignments for innovation include the Stage-Gate™ process and the PMI® project management technique.[1] Waterfall processes of Figure 3-1 are discussed next and a discussion of Agile methodologies follows later.

---

[1] Stage-Gate™ is a trademark of Stage-Gate International. PMI® is a registered trademark of the Project Management Institute.

*THE STAGE-GATE™ PROCESS*

## Q4: What is the Stage-Gate™ process?

A4: The Stage-Gate™ process for innovation project management is perhaps the oldest and most widely implemented system to manage the transformation of an idea into a commercial product [2]. Designing and developing a product, service, application, program, or system using the Stage-Gate process involves making small investments during the earliest stages (called the *front end of innovation*) where risk is low. Increased development expenses occur as knowledge about the markets and technologies is improved through specific work activities thereby balancing risk and investment.

An example of a staged-and-gated innovation process is shown in Figure 3-2 where the rectangles represent stages of work and diamonds represent the gates. The light bulb indicates a new idea entering the process and the circle indicates that the product has been commercialized with all post-launch and lessons learned reviews completed. Work on the project effort is done in stages while decisions are made at gate reviews.

Some common innovation stages, as shown in Figure 3-2 include the following.

- **Stage 1:** Opportunity Identification
- **Stage 2:** Concept Generation
- **Stage 3:** Concept Selection
- **Stage 4:** Technical Development
- **Stage 5:** Product Launch and Commercialization

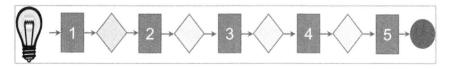

*Figure 3-2: Example of a Staged-and-Gated Innovation Process*

## Q5: What is a stage?

A5: Each innovation stage is distinguished by a separate time period. Usually, the innovation team completes all work in prior stages before moving to tasks in a subsequent stage. However, work does not automatically flow to the next stage since the gate review serves as a decision point to continue or abandon the project.

In each stage, specific work tasks are undertaken by the project team. Each company determines activities that must be completed in each stage, though commonalities exist across all successful NPD programs. Typically, earlier stages (e.g. Stages 1 through 3) involve discovery work, while the later stages (e.g. Stages 4 and 5) include large-scale design, development, prototype testing, scale-up, manufacturing, market verification, and commercialization of the product into the marketplace. Every organization establishes common tasks and activities for each stage of work while each project also includes specific tasks and activities for the unique product development effort.

Note that as a product advances through these stages, more information is gathered from both technical and market perspectives. As more knowledge is acquired, risk is decreased to balance the increased investment in product development work. Normally, the number of team members also increases as the project advances from one stage to the next.

## Q6: What is the front end of innovation?

A6: Frequently called the *fuzzy front end*, the *front end of innovation (FEI)* is a critical starting point where opportunities are identified, and concepts are investigated prior to the more formal stages of technical development and commercialization. Front end NPD processes include the stages of idea generation, initial concept development, and high-level strategic alignment. The FEI starts with discovering opportunities and generating raw ideas for product innovation; this phase is concluded when a formal decision is made to advance an NPD project to detailed engineering [3]. Different skills are needed to successfully navigate the FEI and team members with expertise in front end activities often do not participate in later product development stages.

## Q7: What is a gate?

A7:    Gates reflect the decision point after the new product development work has been completed in a prior stage.  The purpose of a gate review is to approve the go-forward plan for the next phase of development work.    There are three separate results of that decision:  Go, No-Go, or Redirect.

- **Go Decision:**  A "go" decision authorizes the project leader to invest the approved resources to advance the development of the new product project through the next stage.  Gatekeepers authorize expenditures and agree to a set of deliverables for the product in the next stage.  The "go" decision validates that the project meets strategic objectives.
- **No-Go Decision:**  A "no-go" decision means that the project will be halted, often referred to as a "kill" decision.  There are many reasons for a "no-go" decision, such as the product failing to meet expected customer needs, realignment of the strategy, or inconsistent financial outlooks.  A post-launch review of the project is completed to transfer and build organizational knowledge; however, no additional testing or development is authorized.  Product portfolio information, reflecting the entire set of active innovation projects, is updated to show that the project has ended.
- **Redirect Decision:**  The "redirect" decision should be used sparingly, if at all.   In the most common form, a redirect decision involves repeating a portion of work from an earlier stage to gather higher quality or more detailed information for the new product project.  This is sometimes called a "recycle" decision.  Projects may also be put on "hold" due to special circumstances, such as when market seeding for the new product is not complete or if there are not enough resources available for the project to be staffed appropriately.  An NPD

project cannot be on hold for any significant length of time due to the dynamic nature of the innovation environment and commercial marketplaces, particularly with rapid changes in today's markets and technologies.

## Q8: What is the role of a gatekeeper?

A8: Gatekeepers evaluate projects based on the quality of execution of the prior stage of work and make the decisions whether to advance a project to the next stage. Generally, gatekeepers are mid-level managers with the knowledge and expertise in the brand, category, or product area and have the budgetary authority to approve resources for the next stage of innovation work. A focus of all gate decisions is alignment of the NPD project with the organization's business and innovation strategies. Projects must meet basic gate criteria to gain gate approval.

As projects advance through the staged-and-gated innovation process, the investment for the subsequent stage of work increases, often beyond the approval authority of a single functional manager. In such situations, project decisions are made by a cross-functional group that evaluates the potential success of the project from financial, market, and technical perspectives.

Effective gatekeepers are trained for success in the following areas:

- Fluent in the NPD process, including work expected for each stage;
- Deep understanding of strategic objectives;
- Ability to prioritize multiple projects and their goals;
- Consistent application of decision criteria; and
- Skill and expertise in timely decision-making.

## Q9: What are some typical gate criteria?

A9: Innovation project leaders, team members, and senior management coordinate gate criteria prior to each subsequent stage. Several gate criteria are evaluated at each review to validate that the

NPD project remains aligned with the strategy and meets customer needs. Other gate criteria are specific to the goals and objectives of the individual project.

The senior management team responsible for innovation strategy and for making product portfolio decisions outline a set of decision criteria for the project gates. Some typical gate criteria used within an NPD process are listed below.

- Does the project fit with the overall business strategy? Is there a direct linkage to the innovation strategy?
- Does the product support global initiatives or is the market limited?
- Is there a clearly defined customer need?
- Is the market attractive? Who are direct and indirect competitors?
- Are there growth opportunities in the market? Does the new product offer competitive advantage?
- Is the project technically feasible? Do we need to acquire technology or resources to complete the product development work?
- Does the project leverage core competencies? Does the project balance risk, reward, and investment?
- Are there any special health, environmental, or safety considerations? What is the outlook for regulatory or legislative actions impacting the market or product technology?
- What is the risk vs. return and cost vs. benefit? Is the overall life cycle profitability attractive? When are expected financial returns occurring?
- Are they any showstoppers or killer variables that could derail this project? What risk management and mitigation steps are in place?
- Who are the alliance partners, suppliers, and distributors?

Gate criteria are presented as a checklist for the gatekeepers to complete on an individual basis or as a group. If the gatekeepers all agree that the gate criteria are met, including deliverables and resource plans for the next stage of development work, then the project will advance to the next stage. The project is given a "go" decision.

**Q10:  What is the post-launch review?**

A10:  A *post-launch review* (PLR) evaluates the effectiveness of the project team and processes as well as the success of the product in the marketplace.  As in any lessons learned review, the PLR focuses on learning and improving by asking what went well on the project, what practices or policies did not serve the team or project well, and what could be improved next time.  This feedback provides improvements to the staged-and-gated process as well as to decision-making processes for the gatekeepers and the portfolio management team.

The first post-launch review (PLR-1) is conducted at the time that the product is commercialized.  The purpose of PLR-1 is to generate learnings from the NPD team, such as behaviors and processes that were particularly successful (or not) in executing the innovation effort. PLR-1 focuses on people and processes leading to improvements in the staged-and-gated NPD approach.

PLR-2 and PLR-3 are more focused on the success of the product in the marketplace.  Depending on the life cycle of the product, some companies skip the PLR-2.  In addition to evaluating what went well and opportunities for improvement, these later post-launch reviews examine customer acceptance, sales revenue, and other market elements for the new product.  The PLR-2 is deployed for products with longer sales cycles so that more rapid adjustments are made in the marketing and sales of the new product.  Typically, the PLR-2 is conducted about six months after product launch and the PLR-3 is conducted after one year or the completion of one sales cycle.

**Q11:  When should the Stage-Gate™ model be applied to innovation?**

A11:  As indicated in Figure 3-1, staged-and-gated project management frameworks are defined as waterfall processes with serial team management.    Innovation projects that are well suited for implementation within this framework include those that have little risk for change during execution and have low levels of complexity. Products developed using a Stage-Gate system may be technically sophisticated or serving broad, global markets; however, the development life cycle is predictable and stable.  Large corporations also tend to favor staged-and-gated innovation processes since these systems provide a high level of quality and consistency for project selection, advancement, and completion.    Planning and estimating staged-and-gated projects are benefits gained by effective post-launch reviews.

*THE PMI® PROCESSES*

**Q12:  What are the PMI® processes?**

A12:   Established in the 1960s, the Project Management Institute (PMI®) serves as the leading trade association for project management. With a mission to provide standards, knowledge, and information for the project management profession, PMI processes are used across industries and around the world.  The PMI processes involve expected tasks and activities through the various stages of project work. Especially for large projects, hand-offs between teams with different skills occur.

A generalized view of the PMI processes is shown in Figure 3-3 with the process life cycle following stages of initiation, planning, executing, monitoring and controlling, and closing.  Note that during execution, the project manager will monitor and control the process to ensure deliverables and milestones are met; thus, these stages are shown in the figure with recycle and iteration.   Due to discoverable new information during execution of the project, the project plan is revised as indicated by the arrow at the bottom of the figure.

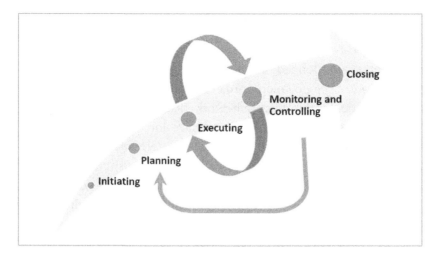

*Figure 3-3:  PMI Project Management Process*

### Q13:  What are key deliverables for the *initiating* stage?

A13:  During project initiation, senior management and the team leader determine the scale and scope of work.  Decisions are made regarding the innovation opportunity and the level of development work required from a technical and market perspective.  Expected outcomes of the initiating phase are the creation of the *project charter* and identification of key stakeholders.

Identifying stakeholders upfront during project initiation has several benefits.  First, the input of key stakeholders, including customers, allows the project scope to be highly focused on specific needs and requirements.  Second, identifying parties with a vested interest in the project directs the team to better understand communication needs for the project.  Finally, the sponsor of the project specifies the high-level budget and schedule, including anticipated launch and release dates for features and products, and aligns the work activity with the strategy.

## Q14: What is the project charter?

A14: The *project charter* is a document that guides the innovation project throughout its life cycle. It details what is included and what is excluded from the scope of work as well as documenting why the project is important to the organization from a strategic perspective. Inputs to the project charter include the following.

- **Statement of Work:** The *statement of work*, often called the "SOW," specifies what the project is expected to accomplish and how the work of the project will deliver outcomes that are strategically aligned with the mission, vision, and values of the organization. The SOW is a narrative description of the project and is very detailed for outsourced work. A description of the expected product is included, such as markets served, technologies utilized, and brand or category of the new product.

- **Business Case:** In order to repeatedly commercialize successful new products and services, each product development project must justify the investment. The *business case* includes strategic alignment of the project with the financial goals of the organization, defines the expected cost-benefit, and establishes boundaries for the project as well as the business need. For innovation projects, the business need typically involves market demand, customer requests, technological advances, legal requirements, and social needs.

- **Agreements:** Any special agreements are also included in the project charter, such as contracts, letter of intent, memorandum of understanding, and any other written agreement that impacts the development of the new product. Legal restrictions in different worldwide markets, especially regarding the privacy of information for customers and other stakeholders, is noted in the project charter. Moreover, the project charter, when signed by the project sponsor and team leader, serves as an agreement for the outcomes of the expected project work.

## Q15: What is the planning stage?

A15: The planning stage is perhaps the most encompassing phase of work for a project team deploying the PMI processes for innovation. Because the PMI processes are waterfall processes, upfront planning is extensive, thorough, and very detailed. A key output of the planning phase is a detailed project management plan that includes the following information:

- Project scope;
- Work breakdown structure (WBS);
- Project schedule, including sequenced activities and tasks and resource allocations;
- Estimated costs and budgets for each deliverable and milestone;
- Quality management plan;
- Risk management plan, including severity of risks, expected financial impacts, and risk mitigation steps;
- Communication plan, including project team internal communications as well as sponsor and stakeholder communications, and external communications with customers and market representatives;
- Change management processes and approval requirements; and
- Procurement management plan.

## Q16: What is the work breakdown structure (WBS)?

A16: The *work breakdown structure (WBS)* is a critical output of the planning stage within the PMI process for project management. It is a hierarchical decomposition of the high-level project deliverables into lower level activities or tasks. Typically, the lowest level of the WBS includes tasks or activities that can be completed by one person, one team, or during one work shift. For innovation projects, the lowest level of work includes items such as designing product components, market research testing and validation, and developing manufacturing processes for the new product. Note that a work shift for an innovation project may span several days or weeks until development activities are completed. A generic example of a WBS is shown in Figure 3-4. Sub-tasks A1 and A2 are the lowest level tasks in this sample WBS. Scheduling, budgeting, and resourcing are completed for the lowest level WBS hierarchy.

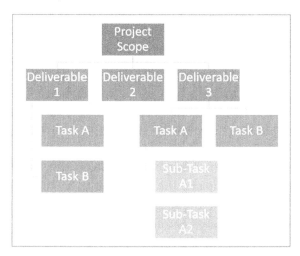

*Figure 3-4: Generic Example of WBS*

## Q17: What is a Gantt chart?

A17: While the WBS shows the tasks that need to be completed for the project, a Gantt chart shows the sequence of activities, dependencies of tasks on one another, and the overall project schedule in a bar chart format. Gantt charts are named after Henry Gantt who first used this scheduling tool after World War II. An example of a Gantt chart is shown in Figure 3-5 where the arrow indicates dependency between Tasks A and B.

*Figure 3-5: Example Gantt Chart*

Task dependencies are critical to scheduling a project. Some tasks have *mandatory dependencies*, meaning that Task B cannot be started before Task A is completed due to physical constraints in the system. For instance, an innovation team cannot test ("Task B") a prototype product until it is built ("Task A"). Other tasks have *discretionary dependencies*, meaning that is preferable that activities are completed in a certain order but there are no laws of physics preventing the tasks from being worked in a different sequence. For instance, an NPD team prefers that quantitative market research is complete before designing specific features, but it not a necessity to do so.

### Q18:  How are budgets estimated for a project?

A18: Estimating a project budget for a new product development effort depends on several factors. First, the scope of work must be clear and concise. Next, the WBS must be comprehensive, listing all activities and tasks necessary to complete the project but no more than those necessary to do so. Third, the schedule of tasks and activities must be realistic and reflect all the tasks and activities in the WBS. Finally, cost estimates for activities must be appropriate and not excessively padded.

Several different methods are used to estimate the project budget. One is the *bottom-up* methodology in which the cost of each activity in the WBS is estimated, including the cost of resources, materials, and labor. Next, these amounts are summed to generate the overall project cost. Estimating the cost of a radical innovation project is difficult and the bottom-up methodology is the best approach.  However, the bottom-up budget estimate is more time-consuming than other project cost estimating methods.

An *historical estimate* uses the actual costs of a similar project and scales to the current project. Scaling factors include inflation, sizing of equipment, number of resources committed to the project, and so on. Historical estimates are generally accurate for new product development projects that involve design of derivatives or enhancements.

Finally, the *parametric* method to estimate a budget is based on scaling a specific parameter or variable in the project. This approach is often used for calculating the manufacturing costs or logistics costs for an innovation project. Historical data must be available for the parametric method to be accurate and the parameter, or variable, must be clearly defined and measurable.

**Q19:  How does the project use a quality management plan?**

A19:  Quality is important to success throughout the innovation life cycle.  The end-product must serve customers with the expected degree of value and reliability.  Moreover, the NPD process must be designed with phases and steps that lead to the highest-level performance of the team.  Quality standards for products are frequently governed by industry or government standards and regulations.

*Quality assurance* establishes which processes and standards are used in the innovation project.  During project reviews, senior management and other key stakeholders verify that the established quality policies and procedures are followed.  In short, quality assurance is doing what you say you will do.

Complementing the efforts of quality assurance are elements of *quality control.*  Quality control includes the measurements and test data, determining that the product meets the established quality standards. Process materials are tested as well as final products.  Thus, quality control is the system that measures output and rejects components that do not meet the predetermined quality level.

**Q20:  What is a risk management plan?**

A20:  A *project risk management plan* is used to estimate the qualitative and quantitative uncertainties within a project and then to create a risk mitigation plan.  The NPD project leader, the project team, risk managers, and other key stakeholders participate in a collaborative risk identification session to identify potential uncertainties that could impact the project.  Such risks include market, technical, and operational uncertainties that influence delivery of the project scope, schedule, or budget.

After project risks are identified, they are classified according to a qualitative assessment by the group. Risks are categorized on the severity of the impact of and likelihood of occurrence. This results in a classification of risks like that shown in Figure 3-6.

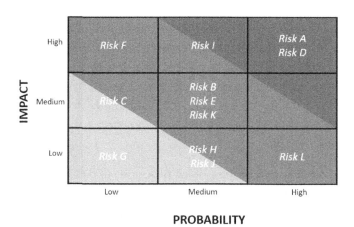

PROBABILITY

*Figure 3-6: Qualitative Risk Assessment Output*

Identified risks that fall into the upper right hand of the impact vs. probability graph are mitigated by re-design or re-engineering of the system. Uncertainties for project tasks and activities that fall into the lower left portion of the qualitative risk assessment chart are often documented without a specific risk mitigation plan due to the low level of impact and of probability of occurrence.

Risks that are shown in the central portion of Figure 3-6 are further addressed by quantitative analysis. The impact of the risk and probability are monetized and prioritized such that the highest impact project uncertainties are addressed with the highest priority. Converting the impact and probability of risk to a dollar amount allows mutual comparison of the risks so that, for example, Risk F and Risk L from Figure 3-6 are on the same scale. More information on risk management is discussed in Chapter 4.

**Q21: How are communications managed for innovation projects?**

Q21: Effective communication is a critical element for success in new product development. Communications among stakeholders must be clear, concise, and accurate. Customer communications build awareness of the new product and ensure that features and attributes meet their needs. Product and technology roadmaps are often used as external and internal project communication tools for innovation and new product development.

Innovation project communications should include both internal and external stakeholders. A communications management plan details *who* receives *which* communications, in *what format*, and *when*. Many project communications are repetitive, such as project status updates, so the communications management plan makes it easier to track information flows and can be used to automate data transfer.

**Q22: How are project changes tracked in the PMI processes?**

A22: During any project, changes are expected. An effective project management system describes how changes are initiated, approved, and implemented. With a waterfall process, changes should be minimized due to the impact on scope, schedule, and budget. Changes can be brought forward from any team member and the project leader estimates the impact of the change on scope, schedule, and budget. Normally, based on the advice of the project manager, a senior review team will approve or reject the change. Approved changes require that the project management plan is updated, including the schedule and budget. Project changes typically result in schedule delays and additional costs; thus, it is important for all team members to be realistic in developing the initial scope of work, WBS, schedule, and budget.

## Q23:  What does procurement management mean?

A23:    Procurement encompasses all project activities related to acquisition of materials, goods, equipment, services, or labor from outside the company.  Most purchases are covered by contractual agreements created during the planning phase of the project. Contracts should include the specific statement of work expected, timing, cost, special guidance, and legal terms and conditions.  The project leader is involved in contract negotiations alongside the legal team.   Procurement of critical equipment is included in the risk management plan.

## Q24:  What occurs during the executing stage?

A24:  During the *execution stage* of the PMI processes, the work of the project is completed.   Key activities include acquiring resources, developing team members, and managing the project plan.   This involves implementing the project communications plan, responding to risks that were previously identified in the risk management plan, and conducting procurements.    During this stage of the project management process, activities and tasks listed in the WBS are completed according to the project plan.

## Q25:   What is the monitoring and controlling phase in the PMI processes?

A25:   Monitoring and controlling the project occurs simultaneously with project execution.  During the implementation of the project plan, the project leader will monitor productivity of the team and progress on tasks and activities to complete the new product.  This includes monitoring the completed scope of work, the schedule, and the budget.

Key outputs from the monitoring and controlling phase of the PMI processes for project management include the status of project, such as percent completed work and work remaining, time spent per task and expected completion dates for all tasks and activities, and project costs-to-date and expected expenses remaining.   When the actual results of the project are very different than those in the project plan, the project leader implements the change management process. Changes are often introduced to adjust task dependencies in order to maintain a given schedule. Other changes may involve new budget requests for additional resources so that the project schedule can be met.

## Q26: What are key activities for the closing stage of a project?

A26: Closing the project is a phase of project management that is often overlooked. During the closing stage of work, the new product is transferred to the division or department responsible for the long-term health of the brand. Production is standardized and team members are released from the project. Final documentation is completed and filed in the company repository. An important activity during the closing stage is to conduct the lessons learned or post-launch review. It is critical to complete the lessons learned review before the team members are released from the project.

Three questions are addressed during any lessons learned review.

1. What went well on the project?
2. What caused significant issues during the project?
3. What can be improved next time?

Just as post-launch reviews provide feedback for the Stage-Gate™ process, the lessons learned reviews provide guidance for improving the PMI® processes. The focus is primarily on people and processes, but successful innovation also depends on balancing project investments with sales revenue.

## Q27: When should the PMI processes be used for innovation?

A27: Like the staged-and-gated model for new product development, PMI processes are best applied for low-risk innovation projects. In particular, the PMI processes serve well as a subset of any other innovation process during construction of plants and factories. With a waterfall methodology, PMI processes are not overly flexible leading to applications where the scope of work is pre-determined with a high level of confidence. Changes to a project is expensive and time-consuming since detailed project plans (created upfront) must be revised, updated, and communicated. However, when the innovation project can be designed within prespecified boundaries and constraints, the PMI processes offer excellent documentation and provide clear expectations for all team members and stakeholders.

## SYSTEMS ENGINEERING

**Q28: How is systems engineering used in innovation?**

A28: Systems engineering (SE) uses integrated, multi-disciplinary teams to manage the life cycle of product development [4]. It is a collaborative methodology combining the application of innovation processes with management, engineering, and specialty functions. Individuals, teams, and supervisors must be skilled in their functions and communicate transparently throughout the development effort. Customers and other key stakeholders have input throughout the SE project.

The SE approach to innovation breaks down the final product according to the "Vee" model as shown in Figure 3-7. Customer needs are a key focus as product design starts with determining operational needs. Following a waterfall process methodology, needs are translated into product and project requirements during the planning phase. These requirements are then converted into design specifications allowing the innovation team to generate prototypes and specific product solutions.

Decomposition of the customer needs through the steps of determining operational needs, developing product requirements, and designing a product solution are followed by the steps to realize the product, service, application, and program. Thus, moving from the bottom of the "Vee" in Figure 3-7, the product is constructed based on design requirements and validated as a solution to the needs described during project initiation. When the product is launched in the marketplace, the innovation team measures customer satisfaction by comparing needs with delivered capabilities.

A benefit of systems engineering is documentation of each step in the life cycle so that all operational needs are included in the design and in the delivered product solution. Version control and detailed designs are tracked throughout the project life cycle which is critical for dispersed teams.

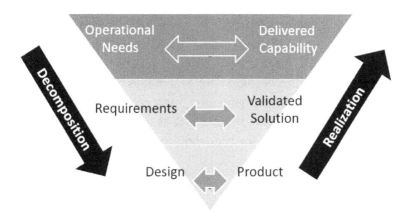

*Figure 3-7: The "Vee" Model for Systems Engineering*

Checkpoints for effective product development focus on the horizontal arrows in Figure 3-7. Thus, the product is checked against the design specifications, the product solution is verified against product requirements, and the final product capability is checked for capability against operational needs.

**Q29: What applications benefit from the SE approach to innovation?**

A29: Because systems engineering is an integrated life cycle approach to product development, it is best used in situations that involve more complex solutions to customer needs. SE delivers more than a tangible product and includes service, application, and sustaining capabilities for the innovation. It is also valuable for virtual teams working on projects that involve frequent change in design specifications. Version control and document tracking help team members, especially those working in remote locations, to manage the development effort. Team membership is generally stable throughout the project life cycle using concurrent engineering that involves marketing, operations, manufacturing, distribution, sales, and engineering and R&D representatives.

Systems engineering is an effective approach to project management for innovation work involving sophisticated customer needs. With the upfront focus on understanding operational needs and developing product requirements based on these needs, SE drives innovation performance. It is important to maintain focus on customer needs without the process becoming overly bureaucratic. Documentation supports collaborative development as a means and not an end. The key benefit of a systems engineering approach to innovation project management is recognizing the product as a piece of a larger system and developing solutions for the whole system in an integrated and collaborative environment.

## *SIX SIGMA*
### Q30: What is Six Sigma for innovation?

A30:   *Six Sigma* projects use integrated project teams with representatives from all functions.   Cross-disciplinary teams are especially important for innovation projects. Because the steps in Six Sigma involve determining requirements prior to starting project work, the process is considered a waterfall approach to project management.

Six Sigma is typically associated with quality improvement yet is effective for innovation projects, especially for companies with a culture dedicated to total quality management. The aim of Six Sigma is to ensure all product and process quality measures meet customer requirements and needs. Product development with Six Sigma follows a six-step procedure [5].

1. Identify product characteristics that customers want.
2. Prioritize product features.

3. Determine sources of product development and improvements (such as design, production, marketing, and so on).
4. Define the process tolerance for each characteristic.
5. Measure and determine existing variations in product characteristics, including performance comparisons to competitors.
6. Adapt the design, product, and processes to achieve a required performance level.

Six Sigma focuses on product improvements by comparing existing performance with desired performance. Customer needs that are not being served by existing products or services introduce gaps that are addressed via Six Sigma product development projects. The Six Sigma project management approach follows the DMAIC method.

**Q31: What is the DMAIC method?**

A31: DMAIC is an acronym representing the Six Sigma project phases as shown in Figure 3-8: define, measure, analyze, improve, and control.

*Figure 3-8: Six Sigma DMAIC Process*

- **Define:** Projects are initiated by defining the product or process for improvement. This can include new-to-the-world

THE INNOVATION ANSWER BOOK

products under development that are designed to fill new market opportunities. A key activity during the define stage is determining customer requirements. Outputs from this initial phase include documentation of the project charter, identification of the cross-functional project team, and listing of customer requirements.

- **Measure:** During the measure phase of a Six Sigma project, the innovation team seeks to understand existing processes, products, and procedures. The multi-disciplinary team develops and evaluates measures of current performance, such as what products customers are currently purchasing to meet their needs and their degree of satisfaction with these existing products. Key outputs of the measure phase include qualitative and quantitative descriptions of current features and products, verified product metrics, and customer satisfaction measures.

- **Analyze:** Data and information collected during the measure phase is evaluated during the analyze stage of a Six Sigma project. This includes detailed analysis of customer requirements and needs leading to a prioritized feature list for the new product or application. Customer pain points are identified to simplify acquisition and use of products, eliminate waste, and build specific new product specifications.

- **Improve:** The improve step is associated with executing the product development work. Critical feature sets are verified with customers and the product or process improvement is designed and developed. Customer feedback is gained through piloting and prototyping new applications and products. Testing marketing plans and finalizing design specifications are key activities during this stage of work.

- **Control:** Designs for products are finalized during the last step of the DMAIC process. A plan for long-term sustainability of the product is created during this phase of work and the product is transferred to the standard functions of manufacturing, sales, and marketing. Key outputs of this stage include identifying new opportunities, especially for next generation feature and product improvements. These activities generate new Six Sigma projects; thus, the DMAIC process is cyclical as illustrated in Figure 3-8.

**Q32: What is Quality Function Deployment (QFD)?**

A32: *Quality Function Deployment (QFD)* is a structured method used in product development processes to link market requirements with engineering design standards. QFD uses a multi-disciplinary team and results of the studies are typically represented with the House of Quality, as shown in Figure 3-9. While the technique is relatively complex and should be implemented with a trained facilitator, the concept of matching customer needs with design specifications leads to a reduction in development time, fewer engineering changes, and reduced cost [6]. All innovation teams strive to match customer needs with design specifications.

Quality function deployment is a mathematical matrix analysis and was pioneered for the automobile industry. There are six sections in the House of Quality that are completed during the QFD evaluation in sequence. Each section comprises a structured matrix as represented by the cross-hatching of Section 4 in the figure.

1. **Customer Requirements:** In Step 1 of the QFD process, customer attributes and needs are identified. This includes understanding market research from surveys and focus groups and translating these insights into statements of expectations from the customer's viewpoint.
2. **Planning Matrix:** In the second step of QFD analysis, the planning matrix is completed. The cross-functional product design and development team considers how each direct competitor fulfills the listed customer requirements. An outcome of the planning step results in a comparison of how well the company's offerings currently meet customer needs in addition to how specific features compare to competitors.

Often, the planning matrix includes aspirational goals to meet or exceed customer expectations.

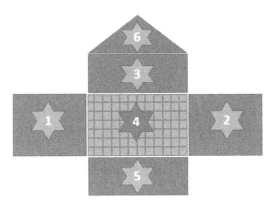

*Figure 3-9: House of Quality*

3. **Technical Requirements:** Technical requirements are product design attributes or characteristics expressed in engineering and operational terms. While customer requirements describe "what" a customer wants, the technical requirements describe "how" the features can be implemented. Technical requirements are specific and measurable. Constructing the House of Quality incorporates a discussion from the cross-functional team regarding the necessary level of accuracy for technical requirements to satisfy customer needs. In addition, as well as the direction of improvement, such as to maximize or minimize engineering parameters of existing product features, is indicated.

4. **Relationship Matrix:** Section 4 of the House of Quality is the key feature of the Quality Function Deployment methodology. The type of relationship between each variable in the customer requirements list is assessed against each of the technical requirements. The matrix is populated with numbers or symbols indicating the strength of the relationship of each pair

of requirements so that any team member can – at a glance – determine which requirements are most critical for the product development effort. Relationships are noted as positive or negative influences between the variables.

5. **Target Technical Requirements:** As the customer needs are compared against competitor features and technical design specifications, a prioritized list of technical requirements is developed. Section 5 in the House of Quality illustrates these priorities and indicates the benchmark specifications necessary for the innovation team to develop and incorporate in the new product design.

6. **Technical Correlation Matrix:** Finally, Section 6 of the House of Quality presents a checkpoint for the new product design. Sometimes, technical features introduce negative or undesired interactions in the final product. The technical correlation matrix evaluates how each technical requirement influences other variables and factors to prevent undesirable relationships among technical specifications for the final product design.

Completing a full House of Quality for a QFD analysis is a complex task and should be led only by a trained facilitator. The mathematics and statistics involved in the matrix calculations are complicated and mistakes influence the final prioritization of product features. Many innovation teams recognize the importance of matching customer needs with technical requirements but do not have the capacity or capability to conduct a full QFD process during the design effort. Focusing on Section 4, the Relationship Matrix, of the House of Quality offers many of the advantages of the method without the disadvantages of complex calculations.

**Q33:  What applications benefit from Six Sigma in innovation?**

A33:  The DMAIC process is well suited for projects that involve product derivatives, enhancements, and improvements. Next generation products that add improvements based on customer feedback are also projects that work well with a Six Sigma approach to project management. Of course, Six Sigma applies well to product development projects that are designed to decrease costs, improve customer satisfaction, simplify usage, eliminate waste, or enhance quality.

*THE AGILE PHILOSOPHY FOR PROJECT MANAGEMENT*

**Q34: What is the Agile philosophy?**

A34: Agile project management processes are based on the Agile Manifesto. The Agile Manifesto was composed by a group of software developers frustrated at the lack of success in product delivery. In order to speed time-to-market, Agile project management approaches add flexibility to the development process. The Agile Manifesto focuses on communication, experimentation, customers, and adaptability. While all elements of the following statements are true, Agile practitioners focus on the phrases to the left more than those on the right [7].

- *Individuals and interactions* over processes and tools
- *Working software [products]* over comprehensive documentation
- *Customer collaboration* over contract negotiations
- *Responding to change* over following a plan

*SCRUM*

**Q35: What is Scrum project management?**

A35: Scrum is the most frequently implemented Agile project management framework and is the most appropriate for tangible product development. Scrum is an adaptive and iterative methodology intended to deliver value quickly and throughout the project life cycle. Scrum is designed to increase customer collaboration, improve communication, and engage cross-functional NPD team members. An overview of the Scrum process is shown in Figure 3-10.

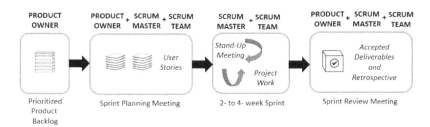

| PRODUCT OWNER | PRODUCT + SCRUM + SCRUM OWNER MASTER TEAM | SCRUM + SCRUM MASTER TEAM | PRODUCT + SCRUM + SCRUM OWNER MASTER TEAM |
|---|---|---|---|

*Figure 3-10: Scrum Project Management Framework*

The product development cycle in a Scrum framework begins with the *project vision statement* created by all relevant stakeholders, including the customer or customer representative. A *product owner* (who represents the voice of the customer) develops the *product backlog* which includes a prioritized list of business and product requirements in the form of *user stories*. The Scrum team members work on just a few of the highest priority user stories during a two- to four-week sprint. During the sprint, team members meet daily in a *stand-up meeting* to discuss progress on feature development. At the conclusion of the sprint, the product owner meets with the development team to accept feature or product deliverables when these meet the predetermined acceptance criteria. A sprint *retrospective* meeting is also held at the completion of each sprint, serving as a lessons learned review to improve team processes and performance for the next sprint.

The sprint work cycles repeat until the project is done, defined as the completion of all user stories and to the determination of the product owner or customer. In this way, the Scrum project management framework ensures compliance with the Agile values of customer collaboration and responding to change. A key principle in executing Scrum projects is timeboxing.

### Q36: What is timeboxing?

A36: Timeboxing is a core principle in the Agile project management framework, especially for Scrum and spiral NPD. The theory of timeboxing proposes a fixed amount of time for each task or activity and ensures that progress is continuously advanced on the project.

Advantages of timeboxing include an efficient development process, reduced project overhead costs, and greater speed to market. Some key activities that are timeboxed follow.

- **Sprint:** A sprint is a project iteration (typically two to four weeks) in which the Scrum team is highly focused on conducting the work of the project. The Scrum master shields the team from outside interference during the sprint so the NPD team can focus only on the project work.

- **Stand-Up Meeting:** Daily, a 15-minute meeting is held by the Scrum team and facilitated by the Scrum master. The product owner is typically an observer, but not a participant, in the daily stand-up meeting. Team members briefly outline what they did the day before, what they plan to do today, and if they need help on any task or in removing impediments to accomplishing work.

- **Sprint Planning Meeting:** This is a 4- to 8-hour meeting (scaled to the length of the sprint) in which the product owner explains the user stories to be worked during the upcoming sprint. User stories are narratives describing the features or attributes of the product under design and are based on the prioritized product backlog. The development team uses a variety of tools to delineate and estimate task durations as they break down the user story into specific activities to work during the sprint.

- **Sprint Review Meeting:** Following each sprint, a 2- to 4-hour review meeting is conducted. The length of this meeting is scaled to the length of the sprint. All stakeholders involved in the sprint participate in the sprint review meeting. The Scrum team demonstrates the product or feature deliverables and the product owner accepts the working increment. Acceptance is measured against completion criteria determined in the sprint planning meeting.

- **Sprint Retrospective:** Like a mini lessons learned review, the sprint retrospective is a 2- to 4-hour meeting that reviews working practices. One benefit of Scrum is continuous learning and improvement introduced by the retrospectives. Team members discuss how they can improve collaboration, tools, and communication during the next iteration. An outcome of the retrospective is an action plan to implement the improvement items during the next sprint.

## Q37: What are the key roles in Scrum?

A37: There are three key roles in Scrum that are mandatory for the success of any project. Individuals assigned to an innovation project using the Scrum framework are responsible for the success of each iteration (sprint) as well as the overall project. Scrum roles include the product owner, the Scrum master, and the Scrum (or product development) team.

## Q38: Who is the product owner?

A38: The *product owner* is the person responsible for achieving business value throughout the project life cycle. A product owner may be the customer or may be representing the voice of the customer by with intimate familiarity with customer needs and wants. The product owner is responsible to clearly state customer needs and requirements, and to justify the business case for the innovation project. Prioritization of features and product releases is a key activity of the product owner.

## Q39: Who is the Scrum master?

A39: The *Scrum master* is a trained facilitator who ensures an effective working environment for the product development team. As a *servant leader*, the Scrum master guides and teaches Scrum practices to everyone involved in the project. A Scrum master acts as a liaison between the dedicated project team and other business functions. Further, the Scrum master works to remove roadblocks, clear hurdles, and remove impediments that could hinder the team's work. Scrum masters benefit from traditional project management training to understand scope, schedule, budget, and risk management practices. However, a Scrum master plays a different role than a conventional project manager in that the former focuses on communication and collaboration rather than monitoring project progress against a predetermined project plan.

## Q40: Who makes up the Scrum team?

A40: The Scrum team, known also as the product development team, NPD team, or innovation team, is the group of individuals responsible for accomplishing the work of the project. The Scrum team translates customer requirements from the user stories into deliverables and working product features. A typical Scrum team numbers less than ten people in order to support team cohesion and collaboration. Therefore, for large projects, small teams hand-off their work to others for integration into the overall product (serial teamwork).

## Q41: When should Scrum be used in innovation?

A41: Many new product development projects are born from ideas with significant uncertainties. With uncertainty in markets and technologies, product development is riskier, and the project will experience more frequent and more significant changes. As the complexity and uncertainty of a project increases, Agile approaches offer benefits that are not available with conventional waterfall project management.

For example, market uncertainty could result in significant redirection of a product development effort. A Scrum process handles this uncertainty through the frequent and rapid experimentation involving customers so that change to the scope of work is accommodated during each subsequent sprint. Likewise, technical risks are balanced by the short development cycles so that functionality is verified with minimal investment. Thus, Scrum is ideally designed for innovation work with high risk, significant complexity, and uncertain outcomes. Scrum is used to develop new-to-the-world, new-to-the-company, and breakthrough products.

*SPIRAL NEW PRODUCT DEVELOPMENT*

## Q42:  What is spiral NPD?

A42:  Spiral NPD is an adaptation of the Stage-Gate™ process that primarily uses functional development in work phases with hand-offs at major milestones.  However, the role of the customer is enhanced with the addition of frequent customer interactions as well as increased experimentation within a work phase.

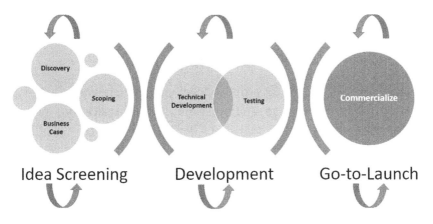

*Figure 3-11:  Spiral NPD Staged-and-Gated Process*

Spiral NPD processes largely resemble staged-and-gated processes with additional iterations during each stage as shown in Figure 3-10. With the adoption of a few Agile tools and techniques to the standard Stage-Gate™ process, the hybrid staged-and-gated model provides a framework for dealing with uncertainty, accelerates innovation, and increases customer satisfaction.  Timeboxing and product delivery increments are techniques adopted from Scrum into the spiral NPD project management approach.

Noting that delivering product increments is different for tangible product development than for software or IT solutions, the hybrid staged-and-gated model considers an increment "done" when work results are completed.  Examples of such deliverables include [8]:

- Market research studies,
- Computer-generated 3D drawings,
- Detailed design drawings,
- Working models, and
- Prototypes.

Spiral NPD builds additional iterations into each phase of work. By adding cycles within each stage, speed-to-market is improved. These iterative cycles are based on the concept of "build-test-review-revise" where testing and revision include customer feedback.

### Q43: When should Spiral NPD be used for innovation?

A43: Spiral NPD is used for product development in the manufacturing sector, food and beverage, and other industries. Applications include those that require higher degrees of flexibility than in the traditional Stage-Gate™ approach, yet outcomes can be defined early in the process. The Spiral NPD project management methodology is best suited to innovation projects that have lower risk, but some phases of work entail higher degrees of uncertainty. In these situations, customer feedback and iterative product delivery help to reduce risk with low investment during the development life cycle.

*LEAN NEW PRODUCT DEVELOPMENT*

### Q44: What is Lean Product Development?

A44: As shown in Figure 3-1, *lean product development (LPD)* deploys an Agile philosophy to project management and integrates cross-functional teams. Like Six Sigma, LPD was introduced through quality management with the Toyota Production System. Quality improvements in a lean manufacturing environment, such as the Toyota Production System, are geared toward reducing waste.

### Q45: What is waste in innovation?

A45: Waste, in an innovation environment, includes wasted knowledge from the perspective of creating new information, transferring data, and application of knowledge for problem-solving. Three categories of knowledge waste in product development are lack of focus, hand-offs, and vague planning [9].

1. **Lack of Focus:** Knowledge is wasted when there is poor communication and when there is the wrong use of tools, including the lack of tools.

2. **Hand-Offs:** In the manufacturing environment, hand-offs create waste due to waiting times. Within innovation, hand-offs create waste when team members do not have access to adequate or appropriate information at the right time.

3. **Vague Planning:** Testing against pre-determined specifications, rather than experiential testing with a customer, creates waste of resources in innovation. The best insights are gained from direct interaction with customers. Another knowledge waste that occurs from poor planning is discarded knowledge, such as data that is gathered but never used.

**Q46: What are the benefits of LPD?**

A46: Eliminating knowledge waste brings cost savings, improved customer satisfaction, and faster time-to-market for enterprises that implement lean product development processes. Improving knowledge transfer among functions and teams also brings significant benefits to the long-term learning and growth of an organization. Some specific benefits of using LPD follow [10]:

- Improved schedule predictability leading to enhanced strategic and market planning;
- Reduced time-to-market for new product and service development yielding lower design and development costs and improved quality in market launch;
- Enhanced flexibility and agility to meet changing customer needs and adoption of new products in global markets;
- Increased productivity of innovation resources as planning and utilization are streamlined; and
- Optimized knowledge transfer internally between, and externally among, product development teams with significant

improvements in capturing and translating cross-functional organizational knowledge.

**Q47: What are the key concepts in LPD?**

A47: There are four key concepts in lean product development as shown in Figure 3-12: cadence, flow, pull, and value creation.

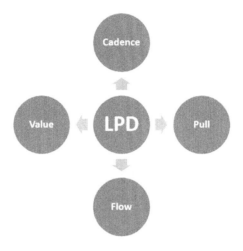

*Figure 3-12: Key Concepts in Lean Product Development*

- **Cadence:** Like timeboxing in Scrum and spiral NPD, *cadence* represents a repetitive rhythm that introduces predictability into the development process. LPD shares techniques like sprints and stand-up meetings with other Agile-oriented innovation processes. Having a certain period of time established between design iterations levels resource usage and reduces waste associated with lack of focus.
- **Flow:** Flow is an important concept in lean manufacturing and in lean product development. *Flow* means that knowledge and materials are available when needed and in the appropriate quantity so they can be handled and integrated into the project. Having a backlog of tasks or excess inventory are wastes in lean. Eliminating these costs to resources improves work patterns, especially in reducing hand-offs and increasing

knowledge transfer. Underutilized talent is another waste resulting from poor flow.

- **Pull:** *Pull* means that resources work at capacity and respond only to customer needs. In traditional project management, resource capacity is often not balanced with project needs – either too few or too many resources are assigned at any given time – creating waste. In LPD, new work tasks are begun only after other activities are completed. A list of tasks is available, including those waiting to be started, work-in-progress, features being tested, and tasks that are done. Usually this list of activities is provided in a central location on a *Kanban board*. Until a team member completes a task, no new activities are added to the Kanban board.

- **Value Creation:** People only exchange money for what they need and value. The lean philosophy builds on this fundamental truth by reducing or eliminating all activities, tasks, and procedures that do not add value to the customer. Many traditional project management systems are bloated with policies, templates, and bureaucracy that try to eliminate risk. Instead, LPD embraces risk as a learning activity and uses experimentation to build knowledge that adds customer-focused value to the product development process.

## Q48: What is an MVP?

A48: MVP is the acronym for *minimal viable product,* a key concept of lean product development [11]. The MVP introduces the minimum set of features that will meet a customer's needs and is developed with the least amount of risk and investment. In this way, customer, market, and technical feedback are attained without excessive waste in development costs, resources, or lost opportunities. Using an MVP as a prototype or early commercial product allows the organization to gain significant knowledge and then target improvements as necessary during later stages of the product life cycle.

**Q49: When is LPD used in innovation?**

A49: Lean product development is applied to all kinds of new product development projects, including radical innovation and incremental or derivate products. For existing products or processes with quality issues, LPD project management is ideal. LPD is also well-suited for projects with uncertainty in markets or technologies, particularly if the development cycles for products or the manufacturing process are lengthy.

---

INNOVATION TRAPS FOR AN ADOPTING ORGANIZATION

- ➢ Not establishing an innovation process.
- ➢ Not matching the new product development process to the risk and complexity of the project.
- ➢ Not training the innovation project team.
- ➢ Pushing later phase work to earlier phases in the hopes of reducing risk.
- ➢ Failing to cancel projects that do not meet strategic goals or when the markets and technologies change significantly.

---

*Then you will understand what is right and just and fair – every good path.*
*Proverbs 2:9 (NIV)*

**Q1:    What are the basics of innovation for a *Transforming* organization?**

A1:    A transforming organization operates with company-wide practices and procedures for individual innovation efforts and aims to take the innovation program to higher levels.  These organizations are gathering and analyzing data to improve new product success in the marketplace and have mature systems to collect customer insights.  A transforming enterprise develops innovation ecosystems to evaluate the overall success of product and service delivery and works to improve collaboration and cohesion of teams.  The goal of a transforming organization is to make better decisions for innovation that increase speed-to-market and optimize value for the firm throughout the product life cycle.  Marketing strategies link innovation to the product life cycle.

## THE 4PS OF MARKETING
**Q2:  What are the 4Ps of Marketing?**

A2: Jerome McCarthy advanced the 4Ps of Marketing which are now a steadfast part of any marketing strategy [1]. These four components are the parameters that can be controlled and directed through a marketing strategy and are inextricably linked to the product life cycle. The 4Ps of Marketing are shown in Figure 4-1 and include product, price, promotion, and place.

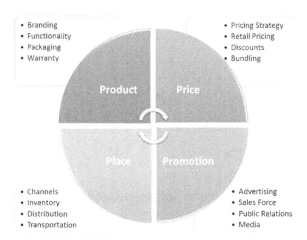

Branding
Functionality
Packaging
Warranty

Pricing Strategy
Retail Pricing
Discounts
Bundling

Product

Price

Place

Promotion

Channels
Inventory
Distribution
Transportation

Advertising
Sales Force
Public Relations
Media

*Figure 4-1: The 4Ps of Marketing*

## Q3: In the 4Ps of Marketing, what does *product* mean?

A3: Some elements of a product include branding, such as the brand name and logo, functionality and features, and styling of the product. In matching a product to customer needs, product decisions include quality resolution as well as packaging and available accessories or services to supplement the use of the product. Finally, product decisions also encompass the life cycle of the product from the customer's viewpoint: warranties, repair and service, and support.

## Q4: What is the whole product?

A4: As shown in Figure 4-2, the *whole product* includes the *core benefit*, the actual product, and the augmented product offered for sale. Note that the core benefit is not a tangible element; instead, the core product is what customers purchase that adds inherent value. Customers have jobs-to-be-done and the core benefit of the product allows that job to be completed. For example, customers buy tape to affix items together or to repair torn paper. They do not purchase tape for the sole purpose of owning tape. The core benefit in this instance is affixing or repairing.

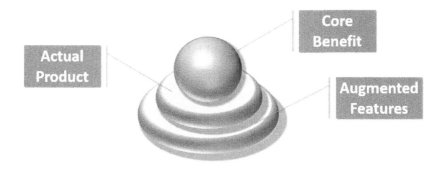

*Figure 4-2: A "Whole" Product*

On the other hand, the *actual product* is a tangible item that is manufactured, distributed, and sold within marketplaces. It can be touched and handled by customers. An actual product must deliver the core benefit and at least match the minimum features expected by customers and of those offered in competitive products. Thus, tape must not only repair torn paper, it must also include a way to store and use the product. A roll of tape that is purchased at an office supply store represents an actual product.

Finally, the *augmented product* provides differentiation among competitive products. Customers will typically pay more for products with special features that aid in their use of the product. Examples of augmented features include delivery of the product, installation, financing, and so. Including a tape dispenser with the roll of tape is an augmented feature for the simple example given.

**Q5: What are the elements of *price* in the 4Ps of Marketing?**

A5: Pricing is generally the outcome of supply and demand. When the supply of a product exceeds demand, prices drop. When demand exceeds supply, prices increase. During product development and throughout the product's life cycle, additional pricing concerns are addressed by the product manager and innovation team.

In any situation, a customer will not pay more for a product than the perceived value. To make a profit, manufacturers work to establish a cost of production that is lower than the price customers pay. When the perceived value of the product is higher, the margin between cost of production and price increases, thus improving profits.

**Q6: What are common pricing strategies?**

A6: Common pricing strategies for new and existing products are shown in Figure 4-3. In addition to supply and demand and customer value, relative product pricing reflects the quality of the product. The four pricing strategies are economy, price skimming, penetration, and premium. Each pricing model has benefits in different applications for new products and during the product life cycle.

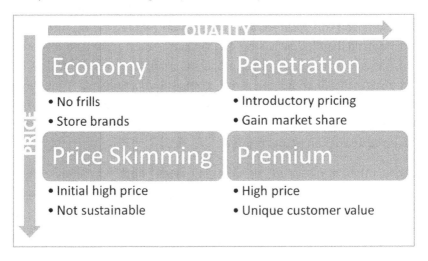

*Figure 4-3: Pricing Strategies*

- **Economy Pricing:** In *economy pricing*, customers purchase products with perceived lower quality because they have very low prices. Products are "no-frills," such as a store brand or generic product with simple packaging. Marketing and promotion costs are kept to a minimum and savings are passed to the consumer.
- **Price Skimming:** As shown in Figure 4-3, *price skimming* represents a situation in which the product has low quality, but the selling price is high. Companies deploy this strategy when

they have a substantial competitive advantage such as early in the product life cycle. However, this advantage is not sustainable over the long-term because the high price and high margins attract new competitors to the market. As competitors enter the market prices fall. Smartphones are a good example of a product that entered the market with a price skimming model. When the Apple iPhone™ was first introduced, it commanded a high price in the market but as competitors, such as Samsung, developed comparable products with similar features, smartphone prices declined and then stabilized.

- **Penetration Pricing:** In the case of *penetration pricing*, a company offers a low price for a high-quality product or service to gain market share. Once they reach an acceptable level of market share, the price is increased. Depending on the nature of competition in the industry, using penetration pricing as an initial pricing strategy risks the long-term impression that customers form of the product. When consumers pay a low price for product, they expect the pricing to be sustained over the long-term. It can be difficult, therefore, to subsequently raise the price of the product after setting a low-price expectation.

- **Premium Pricing:** *Premium pricing* is desirable for many firms because it is sustainable over the long-term and demonstrates customer commitment to the brand. A high-quality product is supported by a high price because it offers a unique competitive advantage. Premium pricing strategies are associated with luxury products, such as hotel rooms at the Ritz-Carlton, first class air travel, and Lexus vehicles.

## Q7: What does *promotion* mean?

A7: How the product will be advertised and promoted are key decisions in a marketing strategy. Firms make strategic decisions to communicate information about the product and about what types of communications are the most effective. Marketing communications include the promotional strategy regarding whether product information is pushed to customers, such as through television and radio advertising, or whether communications are pulled by consumers themselves, such as through YouTube videos or blog posts. Other arenas of strategic importance to marketing decisions include training of the sales force, type and frequency of public relations interactions, and the budget associated with product promotion.

**Q8: In the 4Ps of Marketing, what is *place*?**

A8: *Place* primarily refers to distribution of the product and how the product will reach the customer. Distribution occurs through specific channels that include wholesale, retail, or direct-to-consumer. Companies also consider the point of manufacture and transportation to the point of sale as well as warehousing and inventory decisions. Distribution channels are matched to the quality and customer expectations for the product by ensuring consistency of place with the value proposition. For example, a customer does not expect to purchase a high-quality, luxury item at a discount retailer. Moreover, customers anticipate speedy delivery for online purchases to match product availability through standard brick-and-mortar retail outlets.

## PRODUCT LIFE CYCLE MANAGEMENT

**Q9: What is the product life cycle?**

A9: Just as the seasons of the year progress from winter, spring, summer, and fall, all products go through different seasons in their life. The product life cycle follows a pathway of introduction, growth, maturity, and decline. Since there are no (or very limited) sales during the development stage, it is typically not shown as part of the product life cycle. Product managers and innovation teams make strategic decisions throughout the product life cycle regarding the *4Ps of Marketing* and related product development goals.

**Q10: What are stages in the product life cycle?**

A10: As shown in Figure 4-4, the product life cycle is a sales cycle that starts after the new product is commercialized. Time, as shown on the x-axis, varies depending on the type of product. However, sales cycles are becoming shorter due to increasing product customization, globalization, and pace of technology changes. These factors pressure organizations do more by monitoring markets, technologies, and customer needs closer, requiring more rapid responses to competition.

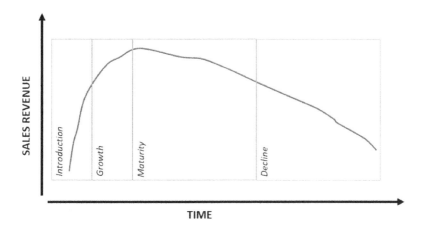

*Figure 4-4: The Product Life Cycle*

- **Introduction:** After development is completed, the *Introduction* phase is entered in which the product is first launched commercially. For new products and services, the goal of this stage is to build brand awareness and develop a market for the product. Sales revenues are not significant as few customers and end-users are aware of or able to purchase the new product. Cash flow may remain negative due to the large investment during the prior development cycle.
- **Growth:** As market share grows, the product enters the *Growth* phase of the product life cycle. In this stage, the organization seeks to build brand preference and to increase market share. Product managers ensure that market share grows enough to balance the investment cost of the new product and that the product offers a reasonable profit margin. The growth period is punctuated by the *break-even* point at

which revenues exceed development costs. As other firms observe the product's success with customers, competition grows.

- **Maturity:** When there is significant competition in the market and most, if not all, customers who want the product are satisfied, the product life cycle enters the *Maturity* phase. Profits remain high for all competitors but will level out with flattening sales, as shown in the figure. Success in the maturity phase depends on differentiation of the company's product from other competitors by adding features, additional services, or other augmentations.

- **Decline:** Finally, as the markets are saturated and technological advances offer new solutions in the product category, sales decline. The *Decline* phase is often difficult to recognize, and companies often fail to generate a market exit strategy until profit margins are unacceptably low. Senior management must decide to retire the product or regenerate it. These decisions are very difficult for innovation teams and product managers who have worked with the target market for a lengthy time period and value the customer relationships. However, extending the decline phase beyond its natural conclusion can be costly to a company in maintaining production capacity, distribution, and advertising.

**Q11: Are there specific actions or decisions in the *Introduction* stage?**

Q11: During the introductory phase, the organization is seeking to build product awareness. This includes branding, setting quality standards, and garnering appropriate intellectual property protection. Sales are initially low since customers are not familiar with the product but begin to increase slowly as the product is adopted. Applying the 4Ps of Marketing to the introduction phase results in explaining the product to customers, educating consumers on the use of new technology, setting a pricing strategy, determining logistics for sales (place), and deciding how to promote the product.

- **Product**: During the introduction stage, companies will focus on creating demand for the new product. Companies need to forge a new connection in the minds of consumers that the new product offers a solution to their jobs-to-be-done. Secondly, the product must be protected against competition and copycats. A firm should ensure adequate intellectual property (IP) protection is in place at the product launch which may include any combination of patents, trademarks, or copyrights. Branding is supported by strong IP.

- **Price:** Introductory pricing can take one of two pathways. First, a company may introduce a new product with *penetration pricing.* Prices are set lower than expected for the quality and demand of the product in the hopes of attracting buyers. Then, as the product gains traction, prices will be increased to match the delivered quality. As indicated above, the risk of penetration pricing in the introduction phase is that consumers may not accept subsequent price increases. Another risk is that a low price often sets customer quality expectations at a low level.

  Alternatively, the price can be set very high, as in *price skimming,* with the selling price higher than the quality of the product demands. However, because there are few (if any) competitors, the firm can charge high prices to address specific customer needs. Price skimming can reduce market penetration as the high price may drive some customers to continue to accept their current product solution, leading to low adoption rates and a long road to profitability.

- **Place:** New products in the introduction stage likely have limited distribution and are not typically available globally. Companies face challenges in distribution during introduction as channel partners want to see profitability before they begin stocking inventory and investing in delivery mechanisms. A direct-to-consumer sales model that is narrowly targeted helps to build product awareness.

- **Promotion:** Advertising and promotion during the introductory phase of the product life cycle is focused on building product awareness. In addition to the various pricing schemes, other sales promotions might offer discounts for first-time buyers or anyone who purchases in bulk. These discount promotions are designed to attract customers to try the new product in hopes of converting them to repeat users.

  Targeted personal selling is another promotional tactic to attract early adopters in a marketplace. Early adopters are key to success of a new product as they are actively looking for alternatives. Moreover, early adopters are often willing to accept a new product solution even if it suffers from some quality issues or lacks a variety of features. These early adopters serve as evangelists for the product by sharing their experience with it as respected experts.

**Q12: How do the 4Ps apply to the *Growth* phase?**

A12: As more consumers become aware of the product, sales increase. During the growth phase of the product life cycle, companies focus on increasing market share by growing demand for the product. With increased demand, manufacturers can reach economies of scale accompanied by increased profits. The growth stage is also marked by increased competition that drives prices down. Innovation teams and product managers design additional features and more sophisticated marketing approaches to differentiate the product from growing competition.

- **Product:** During the growth stage of the product life cycle, competitors arise recognizing the potential for profit as the product gains traction with larger markets available. Companies focus on growing market share and start to differentiate the product against a growing number of competitors. Innovation teams develop new features and product managers add complementary services as differentiating factors to grow their percent of the available market. Offering delivery or installation services (augmented features) can highlight one company's product from competitors as it allows a "one-stop shop" for consumers.

- **Price:** Prices begin to stabilize during the growth phase, especially in comparison to the introductory stage of the product life cycle. If a firm introduced the product with a high price (skimming), then it will seek to maintain that price. In other instances, companies raise the price above competitors to differentiate quality and service. A risk with such a *premium pricing* model is that if customers do not agree with the perceived value proposition, they will purchase the product from a less expensive competitor.

In general, competition puts downward pressure on prices during the growth phase. However, economies of scale result in lower manufacturing costs driving profits higher. In many cases, firms see their first profits during the growth phase as sales volumes increase substantially throughout the market.

- **Place:** As a product is purchased by more and more customers during the growth stage, companies seek to increase product availability. Gaining market share is important during growth, so firms add distribution channels. As more customers demand the product, more outlets offer it for sale. Increasing distribution during the growth phase includes adding new sales channels, including direct-to-consumer, brick-and-mortar, and e-commerce.

- **Promotion:** As more customers purchase the product and competition increases, promotions need to reach broader audiences. Direct marketing campaigns expand to include print, radio, and television advertising while addressing broader customer demographics and different market segments. Customer loyalty programs and special offers are introduced to hold market share against competition. The focus of promotions in the growth phase is to stimulate demand for the *specific product* rather than the product category at large.

**Q13: What decisions are made during the *Maturity* phase?**

A13: While sales increase in the growth stage of the product life cycle, sales peak in the maturity phase. Companies begin to focus on next generation product development and promotions to boost sales. New competitors entering the market take advantage of novel technologies with a lower cost structure than existing producers. Firms strive to maintain profit margins during this stage and actively adjust their marketing strategy to achieve this objective.

- **Product:** Competition is fierce during the maturity stage of the product life cycle. Success depends on differentiating the product from competitors to maintain dwindling market shares. Product features are added to encourage existing customers to buy more of the product in a market penetration strategy. Innovation teams use product enhancements to differentiate the product from competition. Companies may also choose to reposition the product during the maturity phase by re-packaging the product or adding new services to the product bundle. Firms seek to create appeal for new customers to purchase the existing product in the current marketplaces.
- **Price:** It is not surprising that as sales volumes peak, prices drop. New competition entering the marketplace during growth and maturity phases increases supply, and with flattening demand, prices decline. Some companies offer pricing discounts to maintain market share while other firms accept that profit margins are not sustainable past the maturity phase of the product life cycle. Many firms tend to shift their focus to address operating costs instead of customers and markets.
- **Place:** As the number of competitors and distribution channels increase, companies offer additional incentives. Retailers may

bundle the maturing product with other complementary products and services. Manufacturers offer expanded product lines and applications to motivate customers to purchase more of the product. The product is generally available through all available distribution outlets.

- **Promotion:** Complementary product incentives are offered as special sales promotions during the maturity phase. A company may offer free services, such as delivery or installation, to differentiate themselves from the competition. Promotions emphasize product differentiation among the high number of competitors but are targeted at operations that minimize cost.

**Q14: How does a company address the 4Ps of Marketing during the _Decline_ stage of the product life cycle?**

A14: As the maturity stage of the product life cycle ends, sales decline substantially. This marks the beginning of the decline phase of the product life cycle. This is a critical time for companies to make tough decisions regarding the product. Regardless of sentimental attachment, products should not remain for sale when production costs exceed revenues with a declining customer base.

- **Product:** When markets are saturated or a product has been replaced by new technologies, the decline in sales is unstoppable. Companies have three options to consider during the product decline phase: revise (reinvest), retire, or sell the product line.
    1. In choosing to _revise_ the product, a firm invests significantly in innovation to revive the product. Product reinvestments include R&D, development, technology, marketing, and manufacturing. An outcome is the introduction of a next generation product.
    2. The second option during the decline stage is to _retire_ the product. Manufacturers withdraw the product

from the market, spending no more money on production, sales, or marketing. Withdrawal does not completely free the company of all costs. Upon sunsetting a product, firms maintain and honor warranties, service agreements, and spare parts supply. Depending on the firm's reach and integration in the product category, these functions may be outsourced.

3. A third, less common option, is to *sell* the product line. However, if the market has gone stale, not many buyers want to invest in the product or product line. Firms realize similar benefits by simply disposing of production assets (e.g. plant, property, and equipment) when the product is retired.

- **Price:** During the decline stage, any remaining competitors try to maximize profits. Despite low manufacturing and distribution costs, excessive supply drives profits lower. Revenues decline due to market saturation and alternate product solutions as demand shrinks. Retailers offer "clearance pricing" to obtain shelf space for other novel products.

- **Place:** As product supplies exceed market demand, the number of distribution channels shrinks. It is not profitable for distributors to stock inventories of declining products and instead they want to clear their inventory. Niche markets, such as specialty stores, unique geographies, and e-commerce sites, make the product available to a small customer base. Some specialty retailers can sometimes benefit by selling a product that is not available in the mass market.

- **Promotion:** Manufacturers, distributors, and retailers offer clearance sale pricing and promotions on products in decline. Any continuing promotions serve only as reminders that product still exists and is for sale. When companies withdraw from a market, all advertising stops. Public relations statements announce the product withdrawal to maintain customer relationships and to tout next generation or replacement products.

## PRODUCT PORTFOLIO MANAGEMENT

**Q15: What is product portfolio management?**

A15: Product portfolio management (PPM) ties innovation strategy to project selection and execution. A senior management team selects the most attractive new product development projects from the suite of available project ideas. Effective PPM ensures active innovation projects are aligned with strategic goals. Balancing risk, investment, and resources are outcomes of portfolio management. There are several common tools to visualize the project portfolio and to assist in decision-making. PPM is a dynamic process and deals with future events.

**Q16: What role(s) does senior management play in portfolio management?**

A16: Because PPM links the selection of active innovation projects to strategy, managing the product portfolio is a task for senior management. Senior management plays several key roles in setting the direction for innovation, defining innovation projects, and allocating resources.

- **Setting the Direction:** In role of *direction setter,* senior management ensures that all active NPD projects are strategically aligned and properly resourced. Key decisions made by senior management include the degree and type of risk that is tolerated for innovation. Often, risk acceptance is determined by the business strategy and factors such as short- vs. long-term returns, industry competition, and positioning of the firm.
- **Defining Product Line:** Defining the innovation project types in the product portfolio is a role that senior management plays as *product line architect.* Senior management defines the balance of projects with higher or lower levels of risk, shorter

or longer payoff periods, and degree of innovativeness. Working on the right group of projects at the right time also ensures strategic alignment for the organization.

- **Allocating Resource:** Finally, senior management is responsible for *resource allocation*. In choosing which innovation projects to pursue, the right resources must be available to work on the projects. Lack of resources (human or otherwise) can delay the commercialization of a product and undermine the success of the project. Resourcing decisions frequently involve financial commitment to staff projects appropriately; thus, resource allocation is a fundamental senior management activity for effective PPM.

**Q17: What are general project types considered in product portfolio management?**

A17: As the product line architect, senior management defines project types within the active innovation portfolio based on risk, market maturity, and technology needs. The four most common types of projects are breakthrough, platform, derivative and enhancements, and support.

- **Breakthrough:** A breakthrough project includes new-to-the-world and new-to-the-company products. Breakthrough products often involve developing new markets and implementing new technologies. These projects are typically higher risk due to uniqueness and novelty. Payoffs from breakthrough projects tend to be longer term and innovation project teams must be experienced and highly skilled.
- **Platform:** Platform projects may also involve the development of new markets or new technologies and develop a system or sub-systems. A traditional *architectural platform* yields a tangible product with interchangeable components. The innovation effort for architectural platform products focuses on cost-effective manufacturing and distribution, including re-use of materials, equipment, and technical know-how.

Automobiles are a great example of architectural platform products since different models utilize the same engine, transmission, and chassis and they are manufactured using the same equipment.

*Online platform products* are like architectural platform products in that a common technology underlies the product. Online platforms serve to link service providers and users through a central program or application. The platform grows as the number of providers and users increase. Often the software and coding used in one online platform are easily transferred to other products. Some examples of online platforms include eBay™ where sellers and buyers are linked and Uber where drivers and riders are matched.

Using a platform strategy has several benefits since the technology and marketing collateral are easily re-used and re-purposed. A platform strategy allows management to make better decisions based on the anticipated extension of the platform and, particularly in the case of architectural platforms, an understanding of when new developments are needed. The risk of developing a platform is higher than for standalone products since the company is banking on returns over a longer time period from the diversified product family. On the other hand, platform products are cost effective over the long run.

- **Derivatives and Enhancements:** Derivative and enhancement products often arise as next generation products or from the extension of a platform. Typically, these types of projects are lower risk since the markets and technologies are understood by the organization. Derivative and enhancement products may add features or attributes to existing products, such as in the maturity stage of the product life cycle. Financial returns for derivative and enhancement products are shorter term and rely on growth of market share or cost reductions to generate profit.

- **Support:** Support projects are projects that must be included in the product portfolio to maintain existing product lines. These projects include operational efficiency, quality improvements, and minor tweaks to products. In some cases, support projects are undertaken to meet competitive threats or regulatory requirements. Generally, support projects are low risk but have low payoffs as well.

**Q18: What are the goals of product portfolio management?**

A18: Product portfolio management accomplishes three critical goals for innovation that align the active NPD projects with strategy and properly allocate resources. These three objectives are [2]:

1. Maximize value of the product portfolio,
2. Balance the portfolio, and
3. Ensure strategic alignment.

**Q19: How is value maximized in portfolio management?**

A19: A new product portfolio is designed to deliver financial results that maximize the company's profitability. Value is defined by both financial outcomes and strategic results of the active innovation projects. Therefore, value is measured by financial and scoring methods for innovation projects.

Early stage innovation projects are measured by non-financial scores since the financial outcomes are unknown. The portfolio management team works with the project leaders to determine if the new product project fits strategic criteria and is expected to generate acceptable financial benefits. Some measures for scoring NPD projects include:

- **Strategic alignment** such as fit with business strategy, fit with innovation strategy, leveraging skills and core competencies, supporting global business unit needs, and rendering balance;

- **Market attractiveness** such as minimum market size, growth opportunities, competitive advantage, meeting market and customer needs, and lack of regulatory or environmental hurdles;
- **Product advantage** including addressing a direct customer need and providing a unique value proposition;
- **Technical feasibility** such as existing organizational expertise, ability to acquire knowledge, technical sophistication and complexity, and manageable technology risks;
- **Sustainability** such as impact of the product on people, planet, and profit;
- **Reward** including return on investment aligned with strategy and risk tolerance and overall life cycle profitability; and
- **Risk** such as manageable uncertainties, minimal unknowns, and no showstopper variables.

Financial measures are used in selecting active projects within the product portfolio and are more effective for products with known boundaries in the markets, customers, technologies, manufacturing, and distribution processes. Metrics, like net present value (NPV), internal rate of return (IRR), return on investment (ROI), and payoff period are used to compare products with dissimilar development and sales cycles by applying calculations based on the time value of money [3]. For example, projects with the highest NPV are selected as most attractive for the product portfolio. Note that financial estimates have wide variability so consistency in the evaluation is critical in making product portfolio decisions.

Project prioritization follows by selecting the highest value projects in the product portfolio and assigning them to active status. Active projects must be resourced adequately for the product to meet target deadlines in development and launch. When all available innovation resources are assigned to projects, no further projects are included in the active portfolio.

## Q20:  What does a balanced portfolio look like?

A20:  Balance in a product portfolio is different for every organization. A balanced innovation portfolio reflects the strategy of the firm and optimizes risk and value.  Balancing the product portfolio is not unlike balancing a personal financial portfolio since investment goals are aligned with short- and long-term risk of various financial instruments.

Visual artifacts, such as charts and graphs, are commonly used to illustrate balance in the product portfolio and many commercial software tools are available to manage the product portfolio.  However, the most important result of balancing a portfolio is the discussion and evaluation by senior management of active projects, their alignment with strategy, and the availability of resources.  This discussion leads to the decision of which projects to include in the active portfolio. Changes in the strategic direction of the firm require rebalancing the product portfolio, just as life changes require the rebalancing of a personal financial portfolio.

## Q21:  Is R&D investment a way to balance the portfolio?

A21:  Varying the investment in research and development is one way to balance the product portfolio.  This is traditionally called "top-down" planning or the "strategic bucket approach".  Spending on innovation is determined upfront by the senior management team and allocated to different business units, brands, or product categories.  Illustrating the R&D budget on a pie chart, such as shown in Figure 4-5, allows the PPM team to match the innovation investment with the strategic goals, risk tolerance, and overall business objectives of the firm.

For the sample R&D budget shown in the figure, the company allocates nearly half of the budget (48%) to support projects and 28% to developing derivative products.  Just 6% of the research and development budget is assigned to breakthrough projects and 18% to platform product development.  If the company has an aggressive innovation strategy that is risk tolerant and seeks to bring new-to-the-world products to market, the R&D spending does not reflect the organizational objectives. On the other hand, if the firm has established a fast follower strategy and seeks stability in its brands and product offerings, the R&D budget appears to match the innovation goals.

Once the budget for the NPD projects has been set by senior management, projects within each category or "bucket" are prioritized according to additional factors such as rate of return, speed-to-market, technical capability, customer need, and so on.

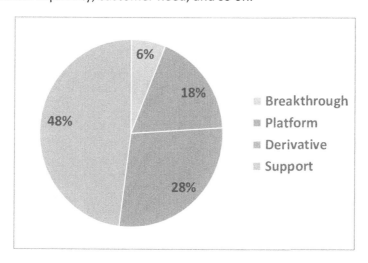

*Figure 4-5: R&D Spending for Portfolio Balance*

### Q22: How are bubble charts used for balancing in PPM?

A22: Bubble charts are commonly used in portfolio management to display the risk, reward, and investment of individual innovation projects on one chart. The axes of the chart are varied according to the critical success metrics of the organization. Risk vs. reward may be plotted qualitatively using a scale of low, medium, and high, or the variables may be shown quantitatively with likelihood of success (percentage) for risk and return on investment (dollars, pounds, or euros) for reward. Often the bubble chart is superimposed on the BCG matrix (see Chapter 2) so the portfolio management team can visualize strategic alignment as in Figure 4-6.

Recall that the BCG matrix illustrates the portion of the firm's market share on the x-axis, ranging from high on the left to low on the right. Growth rate of the market is shown on the y-axis ranging from low at the bottom to high at the top. In the bubble chart shown in Figure 4-6, the size of the bubble is related to the size of the investment. Thus, there is one large project and one medium-sized project in the *star* category. Recall that star projects are good investments since the innovation is expected to bring substantial returns over a long time period.

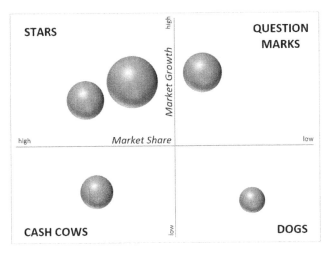

*Figure 4-6: Bubble Chart Example for Product Portfolio Management*

For the sample new product portfolio in Figure 4-6, there are also medium-sized projects in the *question mark* and *cash cow* categories. Investing in projects with varying degrees of risk allows the company to balance its portfolio.

Finally, there is a small project investment in a project deemed a *dog*. This innovation project should be reviewed by the portfolio management team to determine strategic fit. The product could be in the maturity or decline phase of its life cycle and the firm is investing to revitalize the product. In other situations, *dog* projects in the portfolio represent the "razor" portion of a "razor-and-blade" product model in which the hardware is sold at a loss while the replacement parts are highly profitable.

## Q23: What type of chart is used in PPM to visualize portfolio balance over time?

A23: A product portfolio is not stagnant. Innovation projects are undertaken to meet current market needs as well as future growth. The business and innovation strategies establish guidelines for new product projects while product portfolio management is used to select active projects that can deliver the strategic objectives for the firm. Monitoring the product portfolio over time defines whether strategic goals are met and whether adjustments are necessary in the strategy, risk tolerance, target markets, or technology arenas.

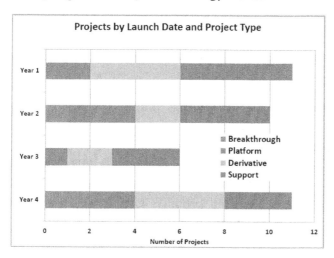

*Figure 4-7: Product Portfolio by Launch Date*

One simple chart for monitoring the product portfolio over time is a bar chart showing the number of projects planned over the near term as well as the types of projects that are in the active portfolio. As illustrated in Figure 4-7, the bar chart breaks down the portfolio by the number of products and type of products planned for launch over the next four years. For example, in Year 2, the company plans to launch one (1) breakthrough product, three (3) platform products, two (2) derivative or enhancement products, and four (4) support projects. The level of innovation risk is linked to the product type since breakthrough and platform products tend to involve more technical and market uncertainties.

A portfolio management team can inspect Figure 4-7 to determine if the balance of product types and future launch date agrees with the risk level and strategic goals expected for the product portfolio over this time frame. PPM teams are also responsible for resource allocation, so monitoring the number and type of products under development and planned for commercialization can yield insights into resource gaps before they occur. For instance, there are fewer products launching in Year 3, which may alert the PPM team to resource limitations in designing and developing new products and services during Years 1 and 2. An alternate assessment of Figure 4-7 may led the PPM team to identify new projects to fill a resource gap in Year 3 and to increase the input of ideas for the new product pipeline.

Ultimately, combining a variety of tools, graphs, and charts will yield the broadest perspective of the product portfolio. The senior management team supporting the product portfolio, along with key NPD process personnel, choose the set of tools that provide the greatest information regarding the product portfolio. Discussion with project leaders, NPD teams, customers, and key stakeholders determines if the selected product portfolio yields the maximum portfolio value at the optimum risk level.

**Q24: What are the key methods for achieving strategic alignment in the product portfolio?**

A24: The chief purpose of portfolio management is to identify, select, and manage product development projects that lead to successful execution of the corporate, business, and innovation strategies. In linking strategy to portfolio decisions, senior leaders address fit, contribution, and priorities of the projects. Each active project in the product portfolio should deliver value and progress toward organizational goals. For example, a medium-term strategic goal for a firm may be to capture larger market share in a given product category. New product projects in the portfolio then should contribute to such goals by adding distinctive and competitive features that satisfy customer expectations.

There are three common approaches to ensure strategic alignment of the innovation portfolio with business objectives. First, in the *top-down approach*, senior management assesses their risk tolerance level and assigns the innovation budget accordingly. Each "bucket" represents various strategic initiatives, business units, or product types and categories. As shown in Figures 4-5 and 4-7, project type is used as a proxy for innovation uncertainty. Using the top-down approach, R&D spending reflects the goals and risk tolerance of senior management since budgets are assigned based on project category.

An alternative method is called the *bottom-up approach* and primarily uses reviews by mid-level management in the NPD process to approve projects in the active portfolio. For example, in a traditional staged-and-gated system, gate criteria reflect strategic fit, contribution, and priorities. However, in contrast to the top-down method, an overall view of funding and resourcing is not necessarily built into project selection. Overall portfolio risk, balance, and corporate objectives may not be specifically considered if a project meets individual gate criteria for selection and advancement.

Companies use the top-down or bottom-up approach to portfolio management depending on the size or number of projects in the portfolio as well as the size of the company and maturity of their innovation systems. Smaller firms may use a more agile approach applying results of lean product development testing to maintain a project in the portfolio. Larger firms may use top-down methods to manage disparate business interests within a multinational conglomerate, for instance.

Many organizations find, however, that a *hybrid approach* to portfolio management is more effective. This combination method applies parts of both the top-down and bottom-up methods to project evaluation and selection in the product portfolio. A hybrid approach is iterative. First, strategic priorities are established by high-level funding decisions for R&D (e.g. the strategic buckets). Next, projects are ranked individually against strategic criteria established by NPD process reviews and where resourcing is assigned. Finally, the combination of individual project priority and resource needs is used to prioritize active projects in the product portfolio.

### Q25: How are decisions made in PPM?

A25: A team of senior executives and functional business leaders meet regularly to discuss and evaluate the entire suite of available innovation projects. Project leaders present current status and goals of individual projects while the portfolio management team compares expected outcomes of these projects with the strategic objectives of the organization. A prioritized list of active innovation projects is prepared to ensure strategic alignment and full resource allocation. Projects are scored with both financial and non-financial methods so that all new product development efforts are compared equally.

### Q26: What is a typical decision-making process?

A26: Decision-making comprises a series of steps that an individual or group takes to solve a problem. In product portfolio management, the problem is complex and requires selecting the highest value innovation projects, balancing risk against strategic and growth objectives, and allocating sufficient resources to each active project. A standard decision-making process involves the following steps as shown in Figure 4-8 and discussed below.

1. **Identify the Problem.** Defining the problem is often the most complicated, but overlooked, element in the decision-making process. NPD projects are undertaken for a variety of reasons, including opening new markets, advancing new technologies, maintaining or growing market share, addressing competitive threats, and complying with laws and regulations. Each

innovation project is evaluated based on its unique contribution to the firm's overall strategy and innovation goals.

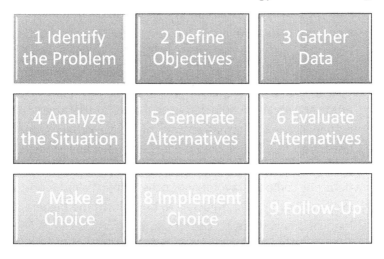

*Figure 4-8: A Standard Decision-Making Process*

2. **Define Objectives.** After the specific problem is identified, the decision-makers define the objectives in solving the problem. In portfolio management, senior leaders are balancing limited resources, time and market boundaries, and budgeting constraints. Other objectives for innovation project decisions include meeting strategic goals for the brand or product family and complying with regulations, standards, and legislation.

3. **Gather Data.** A decision to include an innovation project in the active portfolio is based on objective data and information. This data is available through analysis of the existing product and project portfolio and checklists that demonstrate whether projects meet minimum selection criteria. NPD teams also provide data regarding customer need and feedback, density and quality of the competition, and results of technical experiments and studies.

4. **Analyze the Situation.** This stage of the decision-making process is sometimes called the "pre-decision," or making a decision about *how* to make choices in the portfolio. Both the

THE INNOVATION ANSWER BOOK

problem statement and the data are considered at this phase and the portfolio management team addresses each project's viability and its contribution to the overall portfolio.

5. **Generate Alternatives.** The portfolio management team considers different alternatives for the active set of new product development projects by evaluating risk, balance, and timing. Many of the graphs and charts used within a standard PPM toolkit can be adjusted in real-time so that the portfolio managers view alternative sets of active projects and the impact on risk, timing, and resources. Individual projects may be canceled at this point in the process if the innovation effort does not compare favorably to other projects in the portfolio. Project priorities are adjusted to bring forth the highest value innovation activities.

6. **Evaluate Alternate Solutions.** As different portfolios of active innovation projects are considered, the nature and structure of the portfolio may change. NPD project teams and leaders are informed of individual project decisions that impact the overall risk and balance of the product portfolio. Project decisions are integrated from the top-down (portfolio management) and bottom-up (NPD process) perspectives.

7. **Make a Choice.** It is important to recognize that failing to make clear decisions on the innovation portfolio and individual NPD projects is a risk in itself. Portfolio decisions should be binding, and projects should not be placed "on hold". Each innovation project must meet strategic objectives and contribute to the organization's overall growth and value in a positive way.

8. **Implement the Choice.** Once a new product portfolio decision has been made, the implementation of that choice proceeds rapidly. Team members and project leaders are informed of the prioritized project list within the innovation portfolio, especially regarding investment of resources, expected outcomes, and schedule deadlines. When projects are canceled, team members are reassigned to other innovation projects based on their skills, competencies, and learning and

development needs. Physical assets associated with canceled projects are sold or re-purposed. A lessons learned review of the canceled innovation effort is conducted to optimize portfolio risk and balance in the future.

9. **Follow-Up.** Because product portfolio reviews are conducted regularly (about once a quarter in mature innovation organizations), decisions are evaluated for effectiveness on an ongoing basis. Product post-launch reviews and project lessons learned reviews provide follow-up to the portfolio decision-making process. Learnings from the lessons learned reviews are incorporated for the next portfolio review meeting to ensure continuous improvement.

## Q26: What is the Delphi method for decision-making?

A26: The *Delphi method* of decision-making uses group consensus with a structured communication process. A group of experts is asked to anonymously respond to a survey, problem statement, or set of questions. The process is managed by a neutral facilitator who compiles all responses so that each expert participant provides feedback on all other responses. Next, the prioritized list of responses is sent again to the expert panel who again provide feedback. The aim of the process is to establish a concrete solution by building consensus among the anonymous participants.

Some benefits of the Delphi method for decision-making are that it allows communication for decisions when the normal communication pathways are blocked, it allows disparate visions to coalesce toward one solution, and it diminishes political influence within the decision-making process. A trained and neutral facilitator is critical to success of the Delphi method so that questions and responses are compiled objectively. The Delphi method is also used to investigate ideas and concepts during the opportunity identification stage of a standard NPD process. Because the technique involves written communication, it can overcome some of the disadvantages of traditional brainstorming as well.

### Q27: How does an organization implement PPM?

A27: Research shows that effective product portfolio management differentiates companies that are successful in meeting long-term innovation [4] goals. When NPD project decisions are weak or absent, resources are overcommitted, products miss launch dates, and quality of the development efforts suffers leading to poor customer satisfaction and erosion in market share. Using the hybrid approach, organizations can implement an effective PPM methodology in a short time. Figure 4-9 illustrates the recommended process to implement PPM in 100 Days.

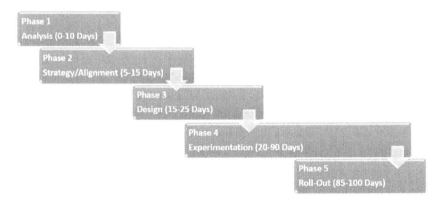

*Figure 4-9: PPM in 100 Days*

- **Phase 1:** In the *Analysis* phase, the current list of active innovation projects is documented and compared to the strategic objectives. The strengths and weaknesses of any current decision-making process are captured so that the current state of the portfolio management system is identified. Gaps and constraints in the current system are noted as are areas for improvement. If a list of active projects is not available, this must be generated during the analysis phase, including the name of the project, significant milestones and due dates, and the names, positions, and commitments of resources necessary to commercialize the product. Project types or categories are identified, if available, such as breakthrough, platform, derivative, or support. The analysis phase typically takes up to ten business days to complete, depending on the quality and availability of existing project data and decision-making criteria.

- **Phase 2:** The second stage of implementing PPM overlaps the analysis phase. Phase 2 focuses on *Strategy and Alignment*. Typically, this phase also takes about ten days to complete as the team identifies appropriate levels of risk, balance, and product mix to meet strategic objectives. Decisions include appropriate ratios of short-, medium-, and long-term projects. Important characteristics of the target portfolio also involve technical feasibility, market attractiveness, capital investment and risk vs. reward.

- **Phase 3:** As portfolio analysis and alignment are completed, a new portfolio management process is designed. Again, this effort can be completed in about ten days. Resource allocation methodologies to ensure project timelines and objectives are designed for repeatable execution in the product portfolio and are realistic. Outcomes of the *Design* phase include an assessment of strategy and risk tolerance, the preferred portfolio evaluation techniques (e.g. financial ranking or scoring methods), suggested visual tools to examine balance and mix (charts and graphs), and decisions on under-resourced projects. Innovation projects that are not resourced adequately are eliminated at this stage or other projects are de-prioritized in order to assign resources to the highest priority projects.

- **Phase 4:** While the design phase lasts about ten days (from Day 15 to Day 25), the *Experimentation* stage is expected to take up to 10 weeks as the portfolio decision processes are tested and refined. At the beginning of this phase, a selected business unit or product family is used to pilot test the decision-making processes of the new portfolio management system. During this phase, the portfolio roles and responsibilities are defined including the direction setter, portfolio architect, portfolio manager, and PPM system owner. Also during the experimentation phase, the selected tools are tested for efficiency and effectiveness in making decisions, the balance of the portfolio is compared to strategic goals, and learning is incorporated from the PPM system users including the senior management PPM team, project team leaders, and NPD teams.

- **Phase 5:** The last phase of PPM in 100 Days overlaps the end of the experimentation stage and lasts up to fifteen days. During the *Roll-Out* phase, the resultant portfolio management system is implemented organization-wide for use by all business units, brands, and product families. Employees and staff working on innovation projects are trained in the new PPM system, including required data inputs and expectations regarding decision-making. Continuous improvement of the PPM system includes productivity and effectiveness of innovation decisions using post-launch reviews, lessons learned, and retrospectives.

## BUILDING EFFECTIVE, CROSS-FUNCTIONAL TEAMS
### Q28:  What is a team?

A28:   A team is defined as a *small number of people* with *complementary skills* that are committed to a *common purpose*, a set of *performance goals*, and for which they hold themselves *mutually accountable*. Each of these terms in the definition of team is important.

Innovation teams must be nimble, flexible, and able to make technical decisions rapidly. Therefore, the core NPD team is limited to six to ten participants, a number consistent with the Agile philosophy. Team members with complementary skills are necessary to complete innovation work since most NPD projects involve R&D, technical development, market insights, manufacturing capabilities, and logistics expertise. With multiple disciplines represented on an innovation team, the work proceeds more rapidly as the various perspectives allow for improved collaboration and problem-solving.

Team members are motivated and inspired to achieve innovation goals by designing success metrics themselves that are consistent with the overall project objectives. Moreover, effective teams build trust that leads to accountability and better project outcomes.

**Q29: What are the stages in team formation?**

A29: Groups develop through shared organizational beliefs and through interactions of individuals. Bruce Tuckman conducted empirical studies of small groups and described the phases of team development [5]. High-performing teams advance through each stage sequentially. As shown in Figure 4-10, these stages are forming, storming, norming, performing, and adjourning. Leaders recognize the importance of team development by supporting communication and collaboration through these stages. A brief description of each phase follows.

*Figure 4-10: Stages in Team Formation*

- **Forming:** In this stage, individuals are assigned to the team or volunteer to serve on the team. The team leader plays a dominant role during this phase because team member roles and responsibilities are not specifically defined. Individuals are selected for innovation project teams based on their work experience, interests, and availability. During the forming stage, group members transition from individual contributor roles in independent functions to collaborative team member roles to create the new product. A key outcome of the forming stage is a common understanding of the project mission and vision.
- **Storming:** The storming stage is characterized by natural conflict regarding roles and responsibilities, project goals, and expectations. It is the primary responsibility of the team leader to manage these disruptions in a healthy way. People assigned

to the team may be frustrated with the pace of development on the team or confused by apparent duplication of roles. Often the problem statement is not clearly defined, and the storming stage is used to clarify the team's purpose and goals. Many teams, especially with weak or inexperienced supervision, can get stuck in the storming stage. Expected outcomes from the storming stage include clarity of roles and responsibilities and clear buy-in to the purpose of the project by all team members.

- **Norming:** Gradually, the team moves from the storming phase into the norming stage. This is when people start to resolve their differences, appreciate colleagues' strengths, and respect the leader's role. During the norming stage, team members establish their own ways of working together and agree upon standard practices. One way in which teams can reach agreement is to document the project goals and team processes in a team charter. In addition to the project charter, expected outcomes of this phase in team formation are working processes, such as acceptable time periods for return of voicemail or email, common software and shared document formats, and collaboration tools especially for dispersed team members.

- **Performing:** The team reaches the performing stage when hard work leads – without interpersonal friction – to the achievement of the team's goals. The team structures and processes, established by the team and including the project charter, are working well. The leader delegates more work to individual team members and concentrates on developing individual team members and skills for the overall group. Team members feel comfortable with each other and enjoy being part of the team. Project work is completed at a rapid pace and learning is at a high level.

- **Adjourning:** All project teams are temporary and disband when the work is finished. In new product development projects, the product is launched and turned over to standard business operations during the adjourning stage. Team members are free to be assigned to other projects or are returned to their home organizations. In some cases, team members are reformed into new business divisions for on-going support of the new product.

## Q30: What are the steps in building an effective cross-functional team?

A29: There are four steps in building an effective cross-functional innovation team. An additional set of tools is recommended for new product development projects using dispersed, or virtual, teams. These steps, as shown in Figure 4-11, are (1) self-awareness, (2) team management, (3) team life cycles, and (4) team processes.

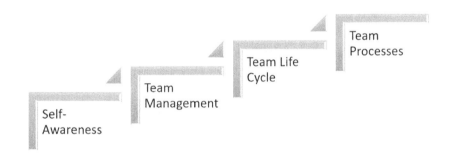

*Figure 4-11: Steps in Building Effective, Cross-Functional Teams*

## Q31: In teambuilding, what does self-awareness mean?

A31: Effective innovation requires open communication among team members and with external parties, such as customers, suppliers, and vendors. Self-awareness lays the groundwork for creating open dialogue. Team members typically complete a work assessment, like DiSC®, to learn what their preferred work style is and to gain an understanding of other work styles. The DiSC assessment highlights biases that can hinder individual trust while providing a vocabulary and framework to improve intra-team communication. DiSC creates a team profile index that allows team members to discuss problems, motivators, and stressors while guiding enhanced dialogue for creativity [6]. DiSC has an advantage over conventional personality assessments (like the Myers-Briggs Type Index) since people's behaviors in work situations is not a pure reflection of personality. The DiSC categories include the following general categories.

- **D-Dominance:** Individuals with a "D" work style prefer a fast pace of work and are frustrated by bureaucracy. They are quick to make decisions and may be perceived as overly demanding. People with a "D" style are action oriented and leaders with this work style preference set high expectations with a sense of urgency.

- **i-Influence:** Team members with an "i" work style are highly energetic and outgoing. They build social relationships easily and seek to engage new people. Some team members may view others with the "i" style as lacking focus; however, these team members add enthusiasm to the team and help build support among outsiders for the work of the team. Leaders with the "i" style offer encouragement and support collaboration.

- **S-Steadiness:** Innovation team members with the "S" work style are considered calm, even-tempered, and do work at a moderate pace. These are valuable traits when the new product development work is chaotic or unstructured and team members with the "S" style easily show empathy for others. While other team members may view their work pace as too slow, these individuals help to stabilize uncertain project activities by building consensus and attending to the emotional needs of all team members. Leaders with an "S" style are reliable, helpful, objective, and tend to be good listeners.

- **C-Conscientious:** The final category of DiSC work styles are people that are analytical and reserved, the "C" style. These team members need to have a complete dataset to evaluate before making a decision. Actions and decisions are based on logic and reason alone. They are often perceived as unemotional but pride themselves on accurate, detailed work. Other team members may view their attention to detail as a hinderance to quickly executing tasks, yet they are very skilled at designing effective project plans. Leaders with a "C" style are objective and emphasize the need for quality work while offering challenging growth work assignments to the team.

In most cases, innovation projects are accomplished with a balance of team member work styles. Diversity of product experience, variety of work backgrounds, and a range of different work styles leads to increased creativity yielding novel product solutions. When team members understand their preferred DiSC® work style and that of other teammates, conflicts in communication are readily resolved[1].

**Q32: What is involved in the team management step of building an effective, cross-functional team?**

A32: Highly productive teams engage in open dialogue and feel safe to both ask for help and express opinions. These are critical characteristics for innovation teams tackling product development with uncertain technologies and unknown markets. Building effective cross-functional teams reduces wasted time and energy, especially that spent on destructive conflicts.

A good teambuilding model is built from Patrick Lencioni's *The Five Dysfunctions of a Team* [7]. As shown in Figure 4-12, foundational to any team is *trust*. After a team begins to build trust, they are then able to engage in *constructive conflict*. Conflict within new product development projects typically involves factors such as budget, schedule, technical alternatives, and market timing. Teams that use constructive conflict management techniques overcome challenges and commit to activities and tasks that move the project forward.

---

[1] Please contact the author at VTM@globalnpsolutions.com for more information regarding DiSC® or Five Behaviors™ work style assessments for your innovation teams.

*Commitment* involves both clarifying tasks and ensuring that the full team buys-in to the solutions.

Figure 4-12: The Five Behaviors of a Cohesive Team™

Once a team has grown through development of trust, learned constructive conflict management, and makes strong commitments to project goals, they become mutually accountable. *Accountability* means that teammates know what to expect of one another and provide honest feedback to keep the project on pace. Finally, building multi-disciplinary teams that work together productively yields better results. Innovation success depends on teams that focus on customer needs and achievement in launching the new product or service.

Teams that complete a *Five Behaviors of a Cohesive Team*™ assessment repeat the assessment after training and practicing the five behaviors. This review motivates team members to continue practicing collaborative behaviors and measures advances in team performance as compared to the initial assessment.

### Q33: How do teams build trust?

A33: Successful teams demonstrate intragroup trust and there are two types of trust necessary for effective innovation team performance [8]. First, *intellectual trust* is an understanding that others are technically capable of doing the project work. Team members validate intellectual trust through educational achievement (e.g. a specific degree or certification), experience, and position or job title.

Second, *emotional trust* is exemplified by not causing another individual harm, offering support to others, and demonstrating selfless behaviors for the overall good of the team. NPD projects with little risk can be completed by teams with only intellectual trust established. However, innovation projects involving higher degrees of uncertainty require emotional trust among team members and project leaders.

Emotional trust is built primarily through relationships. Holding in-person project kick-off meetings allows team members to socialize and begin generating personal relationships that support emotional trust. Agile project management naturally develops emotional trust among team members since each person serves as a generalist-specialist. Following the steps of *The Five Behaviors of a Cohesive Team™* for intact project teams builds trust and offers tools for team growth to optimize innovation results.

### Q34: What is a model of conflict management?

A34: A traditional method of conflict management, shown in Figure 4-13, is known as the *Thomas-Kilmann model* [9]. The first dimension of conflict management is shown on the x-axis as *cooperativeness*. *Assertiveness* is the other key variable in conflict management and is shown on the y-axis. Cooperation is viewed as "concern for others" and is characterized by behaviors to encourage acceptance of views from other team members. Assertiveness is also known as "concern for self" and focuses on getting one's own views accepted by others. By combining various levels (low, medium, high) of cooperativeness and assertiveness, several conflict management styles are evident.

- **Avoiding:** Avoiding, shown in the lower left quadrant of Figure 4-13, is characterized by low concern for others (cooperativeness) and a low concern for self (assertiveness). In many cases , the avoiding style leaves the problem unresolved.

In other situations, a person may assume they are not part of the problem and leave the situation for others, who are closer to the problem, to engage in generating a solution. If the issue is significant regarding the project completion, the team leader intervenes to ensure that the parties do not neglect important or timely decisions.

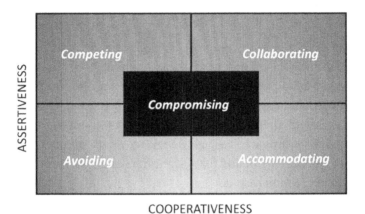

Figure 4-13: Thomas-Kilmann Model of Conflict Management

- **Accommodating:** In conflict resolution, the accommodating style (shown in the lower right quadrant of Figure 4-13) is characterized by a high level of cooperation and a low level of assertiveness. In this situation, a team member may yield resolution of the conflict to others in order to maintain harmony on the team. If team members endorse the agreed-upon solution, the accommodating method of conflict management is acceptable for many issues that arise during innovation projects.
- **Compromising:** At an intermediate level of cooperativeness and assertiveness is compromising, shown in the center of Figure 4-13. In daily interactions, people generally feel that compromising is an effective solution to conflict. Yet, compromise is often viewed as a lose-lose solution since no

one person gained the view for which they had negotiated. Innovation teams may struggle to execute compromise solutions since splitting the difference fails to garner across-the-team buy-in. Project team leaders use compromising as a conflict management technique when the issues are not highly significant. For example, compromising on budget or schedule requests often means a reduction in scope of work.

- **Competing:** Shown in the upper left of Figure 4-13, competing is characterized by a high level of assertiveness and a low level of cooperativeness. It is often considered a direct, but perhaps forceful, way of resolving conflict. The competing style is used to resolve team conflicts when decisions are simple or binary. It is also the preferred method of conflict resolution when safety or regulatory requirements are debated. However, for many decisions within innovation efforts, a competing style fails to consider alternate perspectives that could offer value to the product design effort. However, project leaders that must make time-critical decisions use the competing style.

- **Collaborating:** Many people believe that collaborating is the most effective method of conflict resolution since it involves high degrees of concern for others and concern for self. Collaboration, shown in the upper right of Figure 4-13, requires dialogue among all team members expressing their view of the issue. A fundamental constraint of collaboration for conflict resolution is that it is time-consuming, and it is not necessary for every issue or discussion item. Many decisions for innovation projects can be made by team members based on individual expertise and the goals of the NPD effort.

Managing conflict in project teams requires effective communication and negotiation. The team charter documents the process for escalation of conflicts, especially regarding decisions of resourcing and funding.

### Q35: What are the key roles in the life cycle of a team?

A35: In general, teams are formed and developed according to the Tuckman model of forming, storming, norming, performing, and adjourning. All innovation project teams go through a life cycle including project initiation, acceptance, planning, and execution. Different team members offer strengths to each stage of innovation based on their preferred working style [10].

Regardless of the NPD process selected (see Chapter 3), new ideas are born during the project initiation phase. Successful project teams operate with an open atmosphere and team members are receptive to various perspectives and concepts that will address customers' issues. Individuals that are *Creators* excel during this phase of work because they enjoy brainstorming ideas and are energized by considering a variety of ideas. Other team members, particularly those who are action-oriented, such as *Refiners* and *Executors*, may find the work style of Creators frustrating since ideas are introduced, discussed, and discarded without consideration of how the concept would be implemented into the product design. Each of the roles in the project team life cycle are discussed briefly.

- **Creator:** Generally, Creators are people who generate original ideas and novel concepts. They love the creation process and approach problems with spontaneity, excitement, and energy. Creators focus on new possibilities and have an ability to see the big picture. Team leaders must ensure that creating potential solutions for the innovation project does not become too lengthy of a process or that the team loses focus on the objectives.
- **Advancer:** Much like the "i" work style in DiSC®, team members that are Advancers gain satisfaction from promoting ideas. Advancers, like Creators, often use a spontaneous approach to work but instead of generating new ideas, they excel at placing the new concepts into familiar context. They thrive on recognizing the benefits of novel ideas and tend to be

enthusiastic, persistent, and supportive for concepts generated by the team. Advancers will use the most efficient methods available to achieve the project objectives.

- **Refiners:** Refiners use a combination of approaches to innovation work that are conceptual and methodical. Playing the "devil's advocate" allows a Refiner to challenge new ideas and clarify points early in the process. Other team members may be overly enthusiastic about the ideas and with an analytical approach, Refiners point out weak areas that may not be obvious to others. These individuals play a critical role in the innovation life cycle as they derive risks in addition to the project benefits while ensuring that concepts are feasible, viable, and can be planned in an orderly manner.

- **Executors:** Team members with a strong focus on realities are known as Executors. They are invaluable on the innovation team because they are the ones who actually turn a concept into a tangible reality. Like Refiners, Executors also pay close attention to detail and have a strong desire to see a job through to completion. Individuals with a preference for executing the project often act autonomously and meet project objectives with high levels of quality and professionalism. Many innovation projects would never be finished without the contributions of Executors.

### Q36: What is the Z-model for the life cycle of a team?

A36: As indicated, all innovation projects go through a similar life cycle. The Z-model matches the life cycle of the project with the roles of different team members, as shown in Figure 4-14, where the transitions in the focus of the project work follow a shape like the letter "Z".

In the beginning stages of an innovation project, the team focuses on technical and market opportunities, identified as "Focus on Possibilities" in the figure. Creators are especially well-suited to this phase of work since they enjoy generating new ideas and novel concepts. Teams and project leaders encourage the Creators to express their ideas and welcome unique approaches to solving customer problems at this stage.

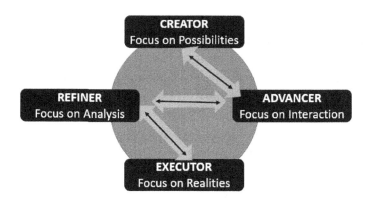

*Figure 4-14: The Z-Model Innovation Project Life Cycle*

As Creators present new ideas, Advancers see the possibilities in these concepts and move the innovation process forward by serving as champions of the ideas. Because Advancers "Focus on Interactions," they ensure that ideas are feasible and fit within the context of the organization's strategy and culture. Advancers promote the idea internally to key stakeholders and verify that potential product solutions will satisfy customers and the external market.

Refiners offer complementary skills to Advancers and excel with a "Focus on Analysis". Teams match the role of a Refiner to the stage of the project in which analysis, refinement, and alternate solutions are proposed. Outcomes at this stage of the project typically include a project plan that moves the innovation into the next stage. Refiners may identify problems with new product ideas, so the project recycles to phases where Creators and Advancers excel at brainstorming and promoting alternatives.

When the basic implementation plan is completed, Refiners present the innovation work to the Executors who "Focus on Realities". At this stage of the new product development project, the tangible work of the project is accomplished. Executors excel during the build and test portions of a project as they are detail-oriented and can pull together multiple tools and techniques to ensure the work gets done.

In an effective cross-functional team, there are no hand-offs between Creators, Advancers, Refiners, and Executors. Instead, team members recognize the phase of the life cycle for the product development effort and allow the individuals with the most skill in a role to lead the project at each stage. Some teams lack representation for all roles and must consciously fill the gaps during the project life cycle by setting aside their work preferences to achieve the project goals. For example, a team may lack an equal proportion of Executors, but all team members will contribute the execution and implementation of the project work to accomplish common goals and objectives.

### Q37: What are key processes for effective innovation projects?

A37: In addition to building cross-functional teams with a foundation of trust, innovation projects document a project charter and manage risks with common processes. The project charter describes the purpose of the project, including how the new product development effort will deliver strategic objectives. Risk management systems provide a set of tools for the team to identify and assess uncertainties for the project.

### Q38: What is the project charter?

A38: In the fourth step of building an effective cross-functional team, team processes move to the forefront. Team members have increased their self-awareness of their preferred working style, team management has improved through trust and commitment to purpose, and team roles are optimized to match natural working styles with the phase of the project. The project charter links the strategy to the new product requirements and provides guidelines and boundaries for the innovation project. For new product and service development, the project charter is called the *Product Innovation Charter* and includes strategic objectives as well as tactical and operational constraints for the project team.

The purpose of a project charter is to document the scope of work, roles and responsibilities, key stakeholders, and expected outcomes. Describing the high-level budget and schedule, the project charter document authorizes the project work to begin and defines the authority of the project manager or team leader. Usually, the project charter is approved by senior management and the NPD project sponsor who is funding the project. In this way, the PIC links specific strategic objectives with the planned activities of the NPD team.

### Q39: What is included in the Product Innovation Charter?

A39: The *Product Innovation Charter* is often abbreviated by the acronym *PIC*. The PIC includes four key sections that define and authorize the new product development project and provide guidance and boundaries to the team conducting the work. A description of each section of the PIC follows.

- **Background:** Every project charter includes the purpose of the project, expected outcomes, and critical success metrics. In the background section of the PIC, the business case for the innovation project is documented indicating how the specific project will fulfill strategic objectives for the firm. The NPD project team will return to the background section of the PIC frequently to ensure that the scope of work is accurately completed. Moreover, the PIC provides boundaries and constraints to prevent over-design or "gold-plating" of the project. If a product requirement is not described in the PIC, then it is considered outside the scope of work for the project.

- **Focus Arenas:** Every new product development project specifies (1) a key technology focus area and (2) at least one target market. Uncertainties in technical and market development are noted for further risk assessment by the project team. Technology development includes whether novel technical solutions are designed for the innovation as well as how technology will be developed (e.g. in-house or via acquisition). Market arenas define market segments, competition, and brand leverage. For new-to-the-world products, market development activities are initiated early in the innovation project to ensure success.

- **Goals and Objectives:** In this section of the PIC, specific requirements for the innovation project are detailed. This includes engineering specifications, budget and schedule limitations, and critical success metrics. Each NPD project must define fundamental measures of success for the new product, including development cost, length of the development schedule, market penetration rates, and expected profitability. Metrics covering both the short-term and long-term are delineated as well as team performance metrics. Successful innovation projects include leading metrics focused on learning and development in addition to profitability, customer satisfaction, and market acceptance.
- **Special Guidelines:** All innovation projects, like the products and services that are developed because of them, are unique. The PIC documents any special guidelines or restrictions for the product development effort. For instance, medical devices and pharmaceuticals require extensive government approvals and must meet strict regulatory requirements. Such legislative and industry regulations are detailed in the special guidelines section of the PIC. The inclusion of customers, vendors, or distributors as team members is documented in this section as well as significant milestones, capital expenses, and requirements involving joint ventures and external stakeholders.

**Q40:  What is risk management?**

A40:  As discussed in Chapter 3, *risk management* is the process of identifying, evaluating, and mitigating the business risk for an innovation project.  Designing and developing new products and services is inherently risky because creating new technologies and building new markets are uncertain activities. However, as a project is planned and executed, risk management processes guide stakeholders, project leaders, and NPD team members to balance uncertainties against cost and schedule boundaries optimizing project outcomes. Risk management starts with selection of the most valuable projects in the product portfolio management (PPM) system and with individual project decisions made through the NPD process (e.g. staged-and-gated or Scrum).

A well-designed risk management process complements the fundamental innovation processes for all NPD projects. Risk management is further linked to the organization's innovation strategy as well as the risk tolerance of senior management. For example, a company with a prospector strategy is more risk-seeking than a firm with a defender strategy.

### Q41:  What are the steps in a typical risk management process?

A41:  The typical steps in a risk management process are shown in Figure 4-15, including identifying risks, qualitative and quantitative risk assessments, and preparing risk responses. Impacts of risk are minimized when uncertainties are identified and addressed earlier in the innovation project. As development of a new product or service advances, risks become more complex and expensive to mitigate.

*Figure 4-15:  Risk Management Process*

### Q42:  How are risks identified?

A42:  NPD projects involve technical and market uncertainties. These risks are primarily addressed through good practices in strategically managing an innovation project, such as product portfolio management and effective decision-making in the NPD process. Additional project risks occur during the execution phases of a project and may require special attention by the project team. Identified risks should be monitored and if the risk occurs, then the risk mitigation plan is implemented. If all potential trigger events for a risk have passed with no occurrence of the risk event, then the item is removed from the active risk management plan.

Project risks are identified in a number of ways. Past experience of the project leader, NPD team members, or other stakeholders determine many risks. Focus groups and interviews with customers and key stakeholders also lead to identification of project risks. Some companies maintain risk management staff, especially in the financial and petrochemical industries; thus, the risk management department notes risks that are less obvious to the project team. A *risk register* is used to document all identified risks, impact and severity of the uncertainty, and any planned risk responses. It is important to assign responsibility for each item in the risk register to a single team member who monitors the trigger events for that risk during the project execution.

**Q43: What is qualitative risk assessment?**

A43: Qualitative risk assessments are used to prioritize identified risks. As described in Chapter 3, risks are analyzed with broad factors of severity of impact and probability of occurrence. Events that are highly likely to occur with a severe impact are eliminated by changing the product properties or the project requirements. The NPD team re-designs and re-engineers the project to ensure that risks with high negative results do not occur.

In fact, the project team will spend the most time and effort in managing risks with either high severity of impact and relatively low probability of occurrence or have a high likelihood of occurring with a low severity. Normally, the project team will then further evaluate these risks quantitatively to prioritize them so that the most severe risks are addressed with a risk response plan.

## Q44:  What is involved in a quantitative risk assessment?

A44:  The purpose of quantitative risk assessment is to analyze project risks so that the uncertainties with the most potential impact are addressed as the highest priority.  As indicated in Chapter 3, priority risk ranking involves assigning numerical values to the probability of occurrence and to the impact.  Normally, probabilities are expressed as a percentage and the severity of impact is reflected in financial terms.  Other quantities are used in various industries and are based upon common measures of risk.  For example, severity of risk in the pharmaceutical industry indicate portions of the population impacted by side effects rather than monetary amounts (e.g. 1:10, 1:100, 1:1000, and so on).

The risk register is updated with the quantitative analysis and prioritized so that the team addresses the highest value risks first.  For instance, imagine that Risk ABC has an impact of $500,000 and a probability of 5%.  Risk XYZ, on the other hand, has an impact of $50,000 and is 90% likely to occur.  Thus, we would prioritize developing a risk management plan for Risk XYZ (potential impact of $45,000) over Risk ABC (potential impact of $25,000).

## Q45:  How is a risk response plan prepared?

A45:  For the highest priority risks, the NPD project team and risk managers create a risk response plan.  The risk response plan is designed to mitigate the impact of the risk event if it occurs.  Trigger events, indicating that the risk is about to occur, are monitored by an assigned team member for each identified risk on the risk register.  When a trigger event occurs, the risk response plan is initiated.  The risk response plan is unique to each identified risk for each project.

For example, a risk identified with the project schedule can be mitigated by adding time to complete tasks in the development effort or by adding resources to ensure that activities are completed on time.  Risks regarding the quality of the product are mitigated by inspection and testing.  Market risks are addressed by gathering additional customer feedback and insights during project execution. Risk responses are realistic, detailed, and documented in the project plans. Thus, if a risk trigger is observed, the risk response plan is immediately implemented to minimize negative impacts on the project outcomes.

## TYPES OF PROJECT TEAMS

**Q46: What types of project teams are used in innovation?**

A46: Traditionally, there are four types of project teams considered for innovation project work. These project teams range from low levels of coordination across disciplines to highly integrated and autonomous NPD teams. The four types of project teams include functional, lightweight, heavyweight, and autonomous (or venture) teams [11].

- **Functional Team:** Functional teams are used for innovation projects when there is a need for depth of knowledge over breadth of knowledge. Much of the work is done sequentially, often by different functions. While the Stage-Gate™ and PMI® processes utilize sequential teams, they often involve multi-disciplinary participation. Functional teams have a narrow focus for product development, such as in support projects or where quality issues are addressed for a next generation product. Depth of expertise is valued in a functional team and team members remain assigned to their primary functional department throughout the NPD project effort.

- **Lightweight Team:** Team members in a lightweight team also report to a functional manager and are primarily assigned to work in a single department. NPD projects executed by lightweight teams typically involve simple product improvements or are derivatives and enhancements of existing products. Lightweight teams typically have a part-time project manager assigned to coordinate the project work; however, the project leader may have a dual role in both managing the project logistics and serving a key technical role. Coordination and communication across functions is increased over a functional team, yet team members may be frustrated by limitations in their ability to contribute to the project.

- **Heavyweight Team:** As the complexity of the innovation effort increases and as the number of team members involved also increase, project teams are identified as heavyweight teams. New products executed by heavyweight teams are tasked with introducing new technologies or launching products into new markets. Typically, a core team of six to ten people serve to make decisions for the innovation project. The core team members are often project team leaders for functional, technical, or marketing sub-teams. New product development projects, such as designing a new platform or introducing a new-to-the-company product, are well-suited for execution by a heavyweight team. Many of the team members serve full-time on the project and it is led by an experienced project manager with a high degree of authority.

- **Autonomous Team:** New-to-the-world products that require significant technical and market development are undertaken by autonomous teams. Sometimes these teams are known as *venture teams* because the products that are launched from the resulting innovations include new business ventures, companies, or business units within the larger corporate organization. Autonomous teams value independence and are often co-located in a separate space than the rest of the R&D functions. In developing breakthrough products with sophisticated new technologies to serve new customer segments, the cross-functional autonomous team focuses intently on project goals. Such teams are led by an experienced project manager and team members are assigned directly to the project rather than balancing functional work and project efforts. Christensen [12], for example, recommends a format of autonomous teams to tackle disruptive innovations. A key challenge for autonomous teams is to reassign team members after the product is launched and the project is completed.

**Q47: Why is transformational leadership important to innovation?**

A47: Transformational leaders inspire change and innovation is rooted in change to improve the interactions customers have with products and services. Organizations that transform to best-in-class performance have leaders that are self-confident, deploy an inspiring vision, are charismatic, and motivate the team to higher levels of achievement. Transformational leaders are effective communicators and are sensitive to the industry and business environment. They provide intellectual stimulation and creative work assignments for themselves and their teams.

**Q48: What are the results of transformational leadership?**

A48: Transformational leadership leads to increased group cohesiveness. Group cohesiveness is a known predictor of group performance. *Group cohesiveness* is defined as the strength of a group member's desire to remain part of the group. Innovation teams that are cohesive display greater levels of trust and are more likely to generate creative innovations that involve greater technical or market risk but have the potential to deliver high value over the long term.

Group cohesiveness is influenced by the severity of initiation, external threats, group size, and mission history. If the group members overcame adversity to become part of the group, that group tends to be more cohesive. The threat of a "common enemy," or competitors for product development, leads to higher levels of group cohesion. Team size is inversely related to group cohesion; larger groups face more difficulty in building and maintaining trust. Finally, when teams have demonstrated past successes, they tend to have higher degrees of cohesion and are willing to tackle higher risk projects in the future.

| INNOVATION TRAPS FOR A TRANSFORMING ORGANIZATION |
| --- |
| ➤ Throwing money and resources at a product that is in the decline stage. |
| ➤ Not matching the 4Ps of Marketing with the life cycle phase of the product. |
| ➤ Failing to realistically value and prioritize innovation projects using a product portfolio management system. |
| ➤ Assembling product development teams without building cross-functional effectiveness through self-awareness and team management processes. |
| ➤ Not identifying the correct type of project team for the level of risk and complexity for the innovation effort. |

# CHAPTER 5

# SUSTAINING

*My steps have held to your paths; my feet have not stumbled.*
*Psalm 17:5 (NIV)*

**Q1: What do *Sustaining* organizations do to maintain innovation success?**

A1: Organizations with one or more successful new product launches seek to maintain their momentum and sustain innovation over the long run. Firms have transitioned from learning about innovation and adopting best practices to transforming their companies with best-in-class processes. To sustain this innovation success, organizations institute learning and growth metrics and nurture leaders in technical and professional performance to sustain their market position and excellence for new product and service development.

## INNOVATION PERFORMANCE METRICS

**Q2: Why are performance metrics important to sustain innovation?**

A2: An old adage says that what gets measured, gets done. Performance metrics gauge the success of the processes within innovation while calibrating the effectiveness of the business strategy. Innovation metrics are used to:

- Support the business and innovation strategies,
- Reinforce critical organizational capabilities,
- Evaluate the financial return on innovation efforts,
- Monitor industry best practices,
- Motivate continued learning among NPD team members, and
- Drive profitable business growth.

Effective innovation metrics allow management to examine new product development efforts in support of the business strategy from a fact-based position, identify gaps in capabilities, and implement prioritized improvements.

**Q3: How is an innovation metrics system designed?**

A3: Organizations that are implementing sustaining elements to their innovation programs implement appropriate metrics that lead to performance improvements. There are four steps in designing an innovation metrics system: defining objectives, planning appropriate measures, implementing measures, and rolling out the system across the organization. Expected outcomes for each step are shown in Figure 5-1.

*Figure 5-1: Design of Innovation Metrics System*

- **Objectives:** Clarifying the purpose of the metrics program is the most important step in designing an innovation metrics system. The primary objective of measuring innovation performance is to determine whether the strategy is successful at the business level and for individual new product development initiatives. Companies competing in the same industry may track different metrics based on different strategies, risk tolerance, internal capabilities, and external relationships. No single set of metrics is better than another since each organization's strategy is different and innovation performance measures must evaluate and validate the effectiveness of strategy implementation.

- **Plan Metrics:** Planning for successful evaluation of innovation programs includes identifying performance goals and determining the current state. Because performance measures drive behaviors, innovation metrics are carefully planned to identify recommended best practice approaches to innovation. Risk-seeking organizations choose measures to drive radical innovation while risk-averse companies select metrics that reflect organizational stability and profitability. Senior management must be careful to limit the number of metrics and to not select metrics without direct links to NPD team behaviors. Often, companies base reward and recognition systems on innovation measures over which project leaders and team members have little or no control.

  A gap analysis is conducted to evaluate innovation metrics currently in place, estimated performance capabilities, and inconsistencies between the current state and desired state. Setting performance goals for new product development programs directs attention to the highest priority and highest value innovation objectives, challenges team members to generate creative solutions, and provides a sense of urgency for strategic new product development efforts. Whenever possible, existing NPD project teams and team leaders are consulted to determine current project success criteria as well as team performance standards.

- **Implement:** During the execution stage of designing a metrics system, senior management and the innovation leaders link decision-making processes with specific input and output measures. Particularly important are metrics used to move projects forward or to halt projects with poor strategic alignment. Responsibility for gathering innovation metrics data, evaluation of the information, and decision-making are part of the implementation process. At this point, innovation metrics reflect the strategic goals and the actions needed to close gaps between current and desired performance for new product development.

- **Rollout:** As with any new or modified system, rollout of an innovation metrics program includes pilot testing within a single business unit, product line, or geographic location. A pilot test of the innovation metrics allows senior management to validate the performance measures and to ensure the system is reasonable to implement across a broad spectrum of new product development projects. For example, data for innovation metrics should be easy to gather, simple to analyze, drive continuous improvement, and support performance goals. The pilot rollout allows minor adjustments to ensure metrics are accomplishing the primary objectives determined earlier in the design process. Once a pilot rollout of the metrics system is validated, innovation metrics are implemented consistently across the organization.

**Q4: At what levels in an organization is innovation performance measured?**

A4: Typically, organizations measure innovation success at four levels, as shown in Figure 5-2:

- Corporate,
- Platform,
- Project, and
- Process.

At these levels, success of all new product development projects is captured to drive strategic alignment and continuous improvement. Different time dimensions, ranging from longer term to short-range, are also evaluated with these varying innovation metrics.

*Figure 5-2: Four Levels of Innovation Metrics*

## Q5: What are corporate level innovation metrics?

A5: At the highest level, firms use innovation metrics to evaluate long-term strategic effectiveness in R&D and in developing new products and services to meet planned objectives. Corporate measures benchmark innovation performance against industry standards and identify opportunities for growth and leadership for the organization. Some common corporate level innovation metrics include the following:

- Capital investment for R&D and innovation,
- Percent of ideas from open innovation sources,
- Product development cycle time,
- Percent of current year revenue from newly released products,
- Number (or percent) of products in the portfolio with greater than 50% market share,
- R&D expense as a percentage of sales,
- Number of new patents filed or granted,
- Innovation team headcount,
- Return on investment (ROI), and
- Break-even time.

Corporate level metrics drive exploration and experimentation while focusing on company growth. Metrics at this level are long-term and demonstrate the effectiveness of the firm's strategy and innovation processes in implementing the strategy through R&D, technology development, and new products.

### Q6: How are platform innovation metrics used?

A6: Platform and product metrics are medium-term and evaluate innovation success through effectiveness in meeting project objectives. Platform and product measures are indicative of market success including identification of the appropriate customer requirements. Often these measures include technical performance of new products, achieving customer specifications, and maintaining design constraints. The general health and maturity of the innovation system is assessed at the platform level by the number of employees who receive training in innovation system management including improvements in the development processes. Some platform and product metrics that are typically used include the following:

- Number of customer needs identified and met,
- Cumulative number of product design changes during development,
- Deficiencies in specifications at various NPD process stages,
- Number of revisions for the product prototype,
- Percent of post-design review changes,
- Life of the product in commercial use,
- Mean time between failures, and
- Unit production costs.

### Q7: How are project metrics used in innovation?

A7: Project metrics are associated with the execution of the product development project and are tied to the specific NPD system used (e.g. staged-and-gated or Scrum). These are shorter range measures that determine effectiveness and efficiency of project management, validating that project risk is acceptable according to the overall portfolio analysis and strategic goals of the organization. Different metrics are applied to each project based upon the project type and risk tolerance of the organization.

For example, a new-to-the-world product creates an entirely new market. Project measures include the degree to which customers accept the new product and that end-users choose to adopt a new product over existing solutions. Likewise, a project introducing a new-to-the-company product measures competitive performance, market share, and profit margin. Customer satisfaction is also an important project measure determining both the short-range and long-term viability of the new product in the marketplace.

Products that are line extensions measure the reach of the product into target markets, how successful the firm is in defending against competitive threats and broadening the product appeal to end-users. Such product improvement projects are typically measured by financial metrics, including sales volume and operating cost reductions to drive profits. If the improvement project was initiated for quality purposes, customer acceptance and lack of defects are also important project metrics.

**Q8: What are process metrics for innovation?**

A8: Process metrics are short-term measures to drive performance improvement during the execution of a project or the next-up product development project. These measures are linked to the NPD process and are often evaluated during project post-launch reviews, lessons learned reviews, or retrospectives. Metrics at the process level measure the success of a project from standard benchmarks such as meeting scope, schedule, and budget. Data gathered for program evaluation supports learning and growth of the innovation teams. Examples of process metrics include the following:

- Project effectiveness,
- Scope of work accomplished vs. planned,
- Time to complete the project vs. planned schedule,

- Cost of project vs. planned budget,
- Project team training,
- Actual resource staffing, and
- Identified product or process quality issues.

Process improvement measures identify areas of improvement during projects so that the project can get back on track if deviations have occurred and to identify best practices for future projects.

**Q9:  How are input and output metrics different?**

A9:  Innovation systems need to balance input and output measures with a focus on continued improvement and learning for innovation teams.  Output measures are *lagging metrics*, defined as data that is collected *after* a product, project, or process is complete.  These measures help innovation teams and senior management determine results of the innovation program, such as sales volume, cycle time, customer satisfaction, and profit.  Output metrics evaluate what has happened in the past and analysis of these measures aids in identification of trouble areas for future improvement.

Input metrics, on the other hand, provide a basis for performance and behavior changes to drive innovation.  These metrics include elements that the innovation team can completely control and indicate the effort needed to accomplish expected outputs.  For example, the number of employees participating in creativity training is an input metric whereas the number of ideas generated in a brainstorming session is an output metric.   To support continuous improvement for innovation, organizations must balance input and output metrics to drive learning and growth.

**Q10:  What is an example of a metrics system for innovation?**

A10:  The *balanced scorecard* is an innovation metrics system that provides input and output measures as well as shorter term financial results with longer range strategic objectives.  As shown in Figure 5-3, a balanced scorecard focuses on four arenas to drive improved innovation performance [1]:

1. Financial dimension,
2. Customer view,
3. Business processes, and
4. Learning and growth.

These four arenas are supported by the organization's mission and vision. Measures of success indicate effective implementation of the strategy.

*Figure 5-3: Elements of the Balanced Scorecard*

### Q11: What are measures of financial performance in the balanced scorecard?

A11: Financial performance is critical to innovation performance regardless of the organization's size, industry, or mission. Without success in the financial arena, a firm cannot meet any other strategic objectives. Shareholders, whether private or public, demand financial strength for investment, making funds available for innovation.

Thus, the financial dimensions of the balanced scorecard determine whether strategic goals are being met, and if not, allow for early course correction.  Some examples of financial measures for the balanced scorecard include:

- R&D investment,
- Profit margin,
- Return on investment (ROI), and
- Target market share.

Financial performance measures align with the organization's strategic objectives.  For example, a firm with aggressive growth goals will include sales volume and market share as important metrics for the financial dimension.  A company focused on operational efficiency selects metrics that drive value creation throughout the innovation life cycle.

**Q12:  In the balanced scorecard, what does *customer view* mean?**

A12:  Customer satisfaction is a key theme for any innovation metrics system.  Within the framework of the balanced scorecard, the customer perspective gauges strategy implementation that, in turn, drives the customer value proposition.  This ensures that product performance, quality, and service meet or exceed customer expectations.  Customers purchase products and engage in long-term relationships with firms when products and services meet their expectations.  Loyal customers not only are repeat purchasers but also share word-of-mouth experiences which strengthens the brand.  Some customer-oriented metrics to include on the balanced scorecard include the following:

- Product return rates,
- Customer complaints,
- Brand equity,
- Return on R&D capital employed,
- Increase in market share, and
- Net promoter score.

In general, these market metrics describe customer profitability, growth, and competitive advantage.

**Q13:  What is measured for internal *business processes*?**

A13:  A balanced scorecard addresses processes, procedures, and policies in supporting strategy through targeted innovation efforts. Business processes address quality, operational efficiency, distribution, and logistics to formulate the company's brand and reputation. Without effective and efficient internal business processes, a firm cannot meet the needs and expectations of customers.  These processes also include the way R&D and innovation projects are selected and executed.  Organizational culture plays a major role in how decisions are made and guide team behaviors.  Portfolio managers, project leaders, and NPD team members take actions that are consistent with the organization's policies and procedures that influence value creation.  Innovation metrics associated with internal business processes include:

- Cycle time,
- Throughput,
- Unit costs,
- Defects,
- Project costs, and
- Process improvements.

**Q14:  How are *learning and growth* measured for the balanced scorecard?**

A14:  Long-term, successful innovation depends on continued organizational learning and knowledge transfer. A measure of learning and growth with the balanced scorecard focuses performance on internal skills and capabilities that support value creation, new product delivery, and customer acceptance.  Learning and growth measures identify potential gaps in staff training and benchmark internal R&D performance against best-in-class innovators.  Some suggested measures for learning and growth include the following:

- Talent development,
- Leadership skills improvement,
- NPD team member training,
- Innovation experience,
- Breadth of innovation skills,
- Creativity workshop participation,
- Employee attitudes, and
- Aptitude for innovation.

Some firms benchmark patents, licenses, and technology transfer agreements to demonstrate learning and growth at the platform or product level as well.

### Q15: What does *surrogation* mean?

A15: Firms must exercise caution in establishing performance metrics. Especially when compensation is tied to short-term metrics, employees may substitute optimization of a metric over the underlying strategic objectives – that is, setting a surrogate of the metric for the strategy. *Surrogation* is a common unconscious bias when the strategy is somewhat abstract, metrics are highly concrete and visible, and when employees readily accept the substitution of the metric in place of strategic objectives [2].

Performance metrics for innovation are intended to make sense of intangible goals and to verify progress toward strategic goals. Innovation leaders counteract surrogation by involving NPD teams in strategy development to emphasize the underlying goals and by having employees establish appropriate success measures.

### Q16: What is the best metric system for innovation?

A16: There is no "best" metric system for innovation across all companies and industries. It is important to design an innovation metrics system that links strategic objectives to performance and team behaviors. An innovation metrics system includes efficiency of the selected NPD process and success of new products in the marketplace.

Having several metrics rather than a single metric aids in visualizing the overall success of the firm with innovation and helps prevent surrogation.

Companies balance risk tolerance with measures of new product development success. For example, a firm that follows a prospector strategy is interested in a vitality measure of percentage of revenue generated by newly released products. A company following an analyzer strategy may track measures of percent of profit from recently launched new products along with operational efficiency in developing new products and services. Defender firms focus on stability of operations and securing high market share. Strategic goals and risk tolerance determine a set of innovation metrics that lead senior management to improve and speed decision-making.

## LEADERSHIP MODELS

**Q17: What defines an effective innovation culture?**

A17: Culture is a set of shared beliefs, core values, assumptions, and expectations of people in an organization. It is an unwritten code of conduct that infers how work is done and is reflected by the stories, customs, and rituals of people in the organization. Effective innovation cultures are determined by the quality of leadership, including communication and trust. A culture in which leaders clearly define the vision and direction through a concise strategy allow the organization's members to be productive and effective in new product development. Innovation success is linked to close and ongoing interactions with customers and team members taking pride in their passion for product development.

**Q18: What roles does management serve in new product development?**

A18: Management plays several roles in innovation and new product development, from selecting the highest value strategic projects and resourcing these projects. Organizations that are most successful with innovation involve management directly throughout the entire product development life cycle. Some management roles are described in more detail below.

- **Champion:** A product champion is a leader that offers support and encouragement for the project, constantly promoting the concept to others. The product champion is deeply involved in the project yet may not have a formal project assignment. Product champions pull people together to ensure that the innovation effort is a success. They are passionate about the project, are persuasive, and are willing to take calculated risks to advance the project. A product champion can help the team gain access to resources but does not provide project funding.

- **Sponsor:** The project sponsor provides funding and formal resource assignments for the innovation effort. Sponsors also serve as guides and mentors for the project leader and the project team, empowering action. A project sponsor often acts as a communication link between the innovation team and other senior leaders, and the sponsor clarifies project decisions if a conflict cannot be resolved at the team level. Normally, the project sponsor plays a key role in laying the foundation for the NPD project including project requirements, milestones, schedule, budget, and resourcing.

- **Process Manager:** Serving as a facilitator for NPD projects, the process manager helps the team improve productivity by minimizing bureaucratic constraints and other organizational barriers. A process manager is well versed in the NPD process used by the organization, often providing training to new team members and ongoing support for existing teams. Process managers are responsible for the throughput of the innovation system and provide governance for all innovation teams. Normally, the process manager participates in all lessons learned and post-launch reviews with an aim to continuously improve the NPD process.

- **Product Manager:** Product managers are responsible for a brand or category within the product portfolio and throughout its life cycle. They act as advisers and consultants for new product development projects by identifying opportunities for the organization to address customer needs and market trends. Product managers help to build brands with emotional attachment and psychological benefits for customers. These attributes go beyond quality and pricing, and product managers are tasked with monitoring customer needs along with matching product development needs to the maturity of offerings in the product life cycle. In addition, product managers provide data and information on both direct and indirect competitors.

- **Project Manager:** Project managers are responsible for the execution of individual NPD projects. They follow the accepted methodology (e.g. staged-and-gated or Scrum) and ensure that milestones are delivered on-time and on-budget. Project managers typically work in a supervisory role yet can provide day-to-day product support for smaller projects. Project managers are fully trained in the innovation processes, portfolio decision-making, and leadership as well as PMI® process for project executives.

## Q19: Is there a difference between product managers and project managers?

A19: Product and project managers play different roles for innovation, yet the roles have some similarities. Both product and project managers have functional accountability and participate extensively in product development projects. Product managers are responsible for the product over its entire life cycle: development, introduction, growth, maturity, and decline. Project managers are typically engaged only during design and development of a new product or service. The product manager monitors and modifies the marketing mix, keeps tabs on competitive solutions, and gathers market and customer insights on a regular basis. Project managers execute and deliver the scope of work to design and develop a new or improved product while carefully managing resources for the project. Product managers provide feedback for innovation projects while project managers direct the work of the team to implement a new product design.

## MOTIVATION AND JOB SATISFACTION

**Q20:  What is Two-Factor Motivation Theory?**

A20:  *Two-Factor Motivation Theory* is attributed to Frederick Herzberg and stipulates that job satisfaction stems from two sources.  These are called *hygiene factors* and *motivators.*  A lack of hygiene factors can lead to *job dissatisfaction* while the presence of motivators can increase *job satisfaction* [3].  In Herzberg's work, people that were dissatisfied with their jobs cited working conditions, pay, security, relations with others, and quality of supervision more than the work itself.  On the other hand, people satisfied with their work quoted aspects of the work itself and of deriving benefits from it.  These elements include opportunities for promotion, a chance for personal growth, recognition, increased responsibility, and achievement.

Managers often manipulate hygiene variables to try to increase job satisfaction and team cohesion.  Yet, providing hygiene factors can only *prevent* job dissatisfaction.  Innovation leaders working on higher risk projects can motivate NPD team members by offering a wider variety of tasks, autonomy, and learning opportunities.

**Q21:  How does Maslow's Hierarchy of Needs apply to innovation?**

A21:  While the Two-Factor Motivation Theory argues that working conditions can provide job satisfaction through external motivation (or lack thereof), Maslow's Hierarchy of Needs argues that people are internally driven to satisfy different levels of needs.  As shown in Figure 5-4, each need must be mostly satisfied for a person to seek the next level [4].  Organizational leaders set the culture and conditions within innovation efforts for team members to achieve higher level needs.

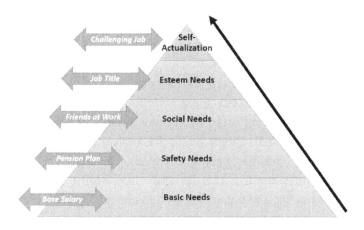

Figure 5-4: Maslow's Hierarchy of Needs

- **Basic Needs:** At the bottom of the hierarchy are basic needs, also known as *security needs* or *physiological needs*. All beings must have basic needs satisfied to continue to survive. These needs include food, shelter, and clothing, for example. From an organizational perspective, survival needs are met with adequate wages and within the work environment. In many ways, these are like hygiene factors necessary to prevent job dissatisfaction.
- **Safety Needs:** When basic physical needs are met, people seek a secure physical and emotional environment. Safety needs indicate people are free from physical threats and are free from worry about money or job security. Organizations deliver safety needs through job continuity, providing insurance, and contributing to retirement benefits through pension plans, for example.
- **Social Needs:** Also called *belongingness*, social needs relate to desires for love and affection and a need to be accepted by a person's peers. Individuals marry, have children, and engage in community activities to meet their social needs on a personal basis. From an organizational viewpoint, leaders promote satisfaction of social needs by encouraging social

interactions and ensuring cohesive teams. Social team-building activities help to promote satisfaction of social needs within company structures. Having friends at work helps to satisfy social needs.

- **Esteem Needs:** There are two elements to esteem needs: a need for self-respect and a need for recognition from others. Status, often reflected by demonstrations of wealth or fame, demonstrates esteem needs for individuals. Organizational leaders address esteem needs through symbols of accomplishment, such as job title, office location and furnishings, and public recognition and rewards. Opportunities for advancement also support esteem.

- **Self-Actualization:** While management supports the culture and environment to satisfy most needs, self-actualization is an intrinsic need that demonstrates a person's potential for growth and development. Achievement and personal satisfaction are reflections of self-actualization. Organizationally, leaders provide opportunities for growth by offering challenging jobs and participation in decisions about their work. Embracing continued learning helps people strive toward self-actualization.

## Q22: What is Theory X and Theory Y?

A22: Management theory also describes the *Theory X* and *Theory Y* model that represents beliefs that managers have about workers. This theory was postulated by Douglas McGregor and describes the assumptions that managers have about workers; these assumptions influence working relationships [4].

*Theory X* is a set of beliefs and assumptions that managers have about workers that is largely negative. People do not like to work and try to avoid work. Managers, therefore, must direct the work of these lazy people and use coercion and threats to ensure tasks are accomplished.

In contrast, *Theory Y* puts forth a more positive set of beliefs and assumptions that managers hold about workers. Work is a natural part of workers' lives and they are naturally motivated to reach objectives when they are committed to goals. People seek responsibility and have the capacity to create solutions to organizational issues.

Generally, and specifically for innovation teams, leaders that follow a *Theory Y* perspective provide greater motivation for team members. NPD teams seek creative solutions to problems and seek greater responsibility, taking pride in their achievements.

**Q23:  What are the typical characteristics of a leader?**

A23:  Successful leaders share several traits. These include a drive to learn and achieve project goals, honesty and integrity, and creativity. Successful leaders are motivated to inspire and lead their teams to higher levels of achievement and are confident in their capability to do so.    Innovation leaders also demonstrate cognitive ability in understanding business, technology, and marketing and have a capacity to quickly grasp challenges and solve problems.  Leaders of innovation projects are flexible and adaptable since the environment for new product development is constantly changing.

**Q24:  What is emotional intelligence?**

A24:  Effective innovation leaders are high in emotional intelligence (EQ).  Daniel Goleman noted that technical competency is necessary but insufficient for strong leadership performance [5].  EQ is comprised of elements involving self-management and managing relationships (Figure 5-5).

**Q25:  What are the elements of self-management in EQ?**

A25:    As shown in Figure 5-5, three elements represent self-management characteristics of emotionally intelligent leaders:  self-awareness, self-regulation, and motivation.  A brief description of each follows.

- **Self-Awareness:** *Self-awareness* refers to a person's capacity for being aware of how they are feeling.  Leaders with a high degree of self-awareness are typically self-confident, have a deep understanding of their own emotions, strengths, weaknesses, and needs. Their decisions mesh with their value systems, and they debate and discuss with a balance of candor and realism. Self-awareness is important for considering the various concepts and perspectives that arise throughout innovation.

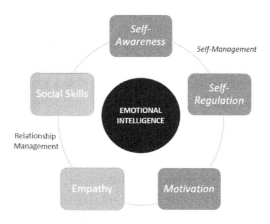

*Figure 5-5: Elements of Emotional Intelligence*

- **Self-Regulation:** Managing emotions includes a person's capacity to balance anxiety, fear, and anger so they do not prevent productive relationships and work activities. *Self-regulation* is the ability to control emotional impulses and to channel bad moods into positive energy. Leaders that refine self-regulating behaviors are better able to cope with change and create team environments endowed with trust, respect, and fairness. Emotionally intelligent leaders practice self-reflection and self-care to enhance their own productivity and integrity. Innovation leaders that have a high degree of self-regulation can resolve project conflicts between ideas, scope of work, schedules, budgets, and resources.

- **Motivation:** Motivating oneself reflects a person's ability to remain optimistic despite roadblocks, barriers, or constraints. Motivated leaders seek challenges, love to learn, and are proud of their accomplishments. Leaders with high *self-motivation* keep score to raise the performance of the organization and are viewed by others as optimistic. Innovation requires implicit technical and market risks, so leaders with a high capacity for self-motivation can support the team effectively.

**Q26: What are elements of relationship management in EQ?**

A26: Empathy and social skills are the two elements of EQ supported by managing effective relationships with others. These are briefly described next.

- **Empathy:** *Empathy* refers to a person's ability to understand how others are feeling, even without explicit descriptions. Leaders with empathy recognize and respect others' feelings, understanding how and when to provide feedback. An empathetic leader responds to body language as well as to spoken words to generate relational bonds. Innovation leaders use coaching and mentoring to increase empathy with team members. Strong relationships with team members improve job satisfaction, performance, and group cohesion.
- **Social Skills:** An ability to get along with others and to establish positive relationships are reflected by *social skills*. Leaders with high EQ exhibit valuable social skills such as an ability to motivate and direct teams. In building rapport across multiple disciplines and functions, team members, suppliers, distributors, and customers, innovation leaders with high social skills can rely upon a broad network to achieve success.

## VIRTUAL TEAM MODEL

**Q27: What is a virtual team?**

A27: *Virtual teams* consist of members who are dispersed in different locations and where communication is primarily electronic. These teams share a common objective, but individuals often work in isolated places or in remote locations. In contrast, co-location is often cited as a best practice for traditional new product development teams following waterfall processes. These teams rely heavily on face-to-face contact and incidental interactions for communication. In comparison, dispersed teams lack face-to-face interactions resulting in different challenges to accomplish innovation work.

Some challenges faced by virtual teams include the following:

- Absence of everyday, non-verbal, face-to-face communication;
- Lack of trust, specifically lack of emotional trust;
- Little or no social interaction;
- Cultural discrepancies; and
- Lack of common fellowship.

While virtual teams face challenges due to the lack of direct, face-to-face communication, there are several benefits in using dispersed teams for innovation work. First, with effective practices, virtual teams can be more productive than face-to-face teams. Virtual team members in different time zones hand-off work so that nearly continuous progress is achieved for project efforts. Next, virtual teams access technical, marketing, and IT expertise around the world rather than relying on local resources alone. Finally, virtual team members bring local market knowledge to the innovation team, enhancing the new product development effort and speeding time to launch.

Virtual teams are identified by team members based in different locations. The degree of dispersion of the team is reflected by the number of team members in each location. For instance, a team that has five members at one location and two members at two other, separate locations has a relatively low degree of dispersion but is highly uneven. Teams located in different buildings at the same campus or on different floors of a building are challenged by the same issues as a formally named virtual team. Any hinderance or barrier to face-to-face, synchronous communication, and a primary reliance on electronic means of communication defines a virtual team.

**Q28: What is the Virtual Team Model (VTM)?**

A28: Implementing virtual teams is a practice within lean product development (see Chapter 3) that reduces knowledge waste to take advantage of all sources of learning and development regardless of geographical constraints. The best and most diverse talent is accessed through virtual teams for product development bringing expertise and cost saving to innovation projects. Effective virtual teams bring an *outside-in* perspective to the project, emphasizing experience, talent, and local market information to improve the development effort by reducing rework and increasing adaptation. Diversity increases creative problem-solving and reduces time-to-market. Lower employee and office costs of virtual teams result in higher profitability for the firm.

As shown in Figure 5-6, the Virtual Team Model (VTM) offers five elements and sixteen practices specific to innovation teams [6, 7]. The first element, *Initiation and Structure*, addresses team member characteristics, team formation, and goal setting. With a higher degree of team cohesion by selecting team members with specific skills and work styles, *Communication Practices* next defines best practices to overcome the lack of face-to-face communication and to enhance technologically-mediated communication methods. The third element, *Meeting and Protocols*, identifies practices to improve communication opportunities and team processes. *Knowledge Management* discusses how the innovation team can meet objectives by sharing information efficiently and effectively. Finally, *Leadership* of virtual teams requires somewhat different skills than traditionally expected for leaders of face-to-face teams.

Leaders and teams improving their virtual teams can start with any element and any practice. Productivity of dispersed teams improves the most when more elements and practices are instituted for team member interactions.

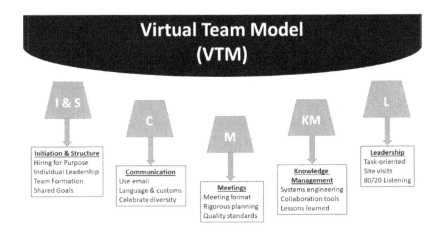

*Figure 5-6: Virtual Team Model*

## Q29:  What are the practices within *Initiation and Structure*?

A29:  Any newly formed innovation team that will be conducting work from several locations and relying on electronic communication should start with the practices of *Initiation and Structure*. Leaders select team members with strong interpersonal skills as well as technical capabilities.  Individuals serving on virtual teams work autonomously with high levels of task responsibility and must be connected to the project mission.  Stages of team formation are largely similar to the team formation process of face-to-face teams yet are established at a different pace.  Finally, the most significant rallying factor to generate high levels of productivity among virtual team members is shared goals, mission, and vision.  Creating a common goal for the team is a driving force for success.

- **Hiring for Purpose:**  Organizations typically have a choice in hiring and assigning workers to innovation projects.  Typical hiring practices center on historical job performance; however, to improve virtual team effectiveness, leaders focus on matching passion for the product with the project goals. Innovation requires enthusiasm for the organization's overall purpose.  Virtual team members with a passion to design and develop the new product overcome inherent barriers of distance, trust, and communication. *Hiring for purpose* establishes common fellowship and interest among team members that, in turn, enhances team cohesion.

- **Individual Leadership:** Virtual team members face social isolation from the rest of the organization and other team members. Yet, they are often tasked with more intense technical development activities. Successful virtual teams select members who are self-motivated and demonstrate strong *individual leadership* characteristics. Remote team members work autonomously while representing the project to local functional management and to the local customer base. Individual leadership is reflected by high emotional intelligence, a factor as important as technical expertise for dispersed team members.

- **Team Formation:** Just as traditional, co-located innovation teams go through specific stages of team growth, so do virtual teams. Following the Tuckman model, dispersed teams form, storm, norm, perform, and adjourn. *Formation of the team* includes all the practices within the *Initiation and Structure* element and especially involves *Hiring for Purpose*. Virtual teams are not as likely to have a difficult storming phase as face-to-face teams, due to the natural autonomy of workers assigned to the project. However, establishing norms can be more challenging for virtual team members who come from diverse cultures and with a variety of standard work practices. Habits and behaviors that are ingrained in some cultures are new and unusual to team members in other cultures. However, as fair and equal policies are agreed by the team members, work performance is extremely high and often outproduces the level of work of a traditional, co-located team. Adjourning is a lesser issue with dispersed team members since they can rely on both local and corporate networks for their next job assignment.

- **Shared Goal:** Commitment to a *shared goal* is the number one success factor for virtual teams. Working with common purpose helps dispersed team members overcome barriers introduced by separate time zones, cultures, and social isolation. The project leader plays a key role in continually reinforcing project goals and objectives, explaining why the team members are working together, and what benefits result from the implementation of the project. Successful leaders reiterate the purpose of the team at every opportunity including team meetings, one-on-one conversations, and formal project communications.

**Q30:  What are specific *Communication* practices in the VTM?**

A30:  Intra-team *communication* can make or break a virtual team. Communication is critical for any relationship to bear fruit. The term "communication" includes both what we say and how we say it. More than 70% of communication is nonverbal so dispersed team members often lose a lot of the message when they primarily use asynchronous, technology-assisted communication methods. However, starting with a basic communication tool (email) and appreciating differences in cultures (language and diversity) virtual teams can be successful in accomplishing team goals.

- **Email:** While email overload is a real problem, *email* is the primary communication tool for virtual teams. Email offers advantages for everyday communication over text, phone, or instant messaging (IM) for dispersed teams. First, email is asynchronous and allows feedback for team members working in different time zones. Second, text messages often include abbreviations that are not readily translated across generations or cultures. Next, phone calls are generally considered a higher priority communication mode and many project discussions do not warrant that level of urgency. Finally, IM conveys urgency to the point of interrupting tasks. It is important to remember that working hours are not matched or overlapping among all virtual team members. Email also gives non-English speakers time to process and respond to information.

- **Language:** English is the primary language of business and is commonly selected for innovation teams working together virtually. Regardless of the primary *language* chosen for the project team, all team members must exhibit tolerance for those not as familiar with it. It is especially important to moderate culturally specific humor and slang since these concepts and phrases can be misconstrued in translation. In any case, if an email conversation does not reach clarity within a few back-and-forth messages, a phone conversation is in order to clarify the written word.

- **Celebrate Diversity:** The biggest advantage of a virtual team is the added creativity, problem-solving, and market perspectives brought by team members with different viewpoints and experiences. While diversity benefits the team in many ways, diversity can also hinder communication. To build emotional trust, innovation teams are encouraged to seek different ideas, methods, and motivations to design and develop new products and services. Sharing cultural norms and understanding differences in work styles improves team cohesion and leads to higher performance. *Celebrating diversity* by sharing and discussing different national holidays, sports, or pastimes enhances team cohesion.

## Q31: The VTM discusses practices for *Meetings and Protocols*. What are these?

A31: In traditional, co-located teams, project issues are often discussed during informal meetings and chance encounters. Casual interactions lead to deeper conversations of project issues such that formal team meetings tend to be uneventful. Project leaders often use team meetings for one-way communication, including status reports on the project schedule and budget.

Dispersed team members need formal meetings to drive in-depth conversations and to make project decisions. Project status and other one-way communications are presented through newsletters, emails, or other electronic tools so that live meetings focus on joint project decisions, technical interactions among project team members, and resolution of outstanding issues. In contrast to conventional project teams, virtual team meetings serve as critical checkpoints. Best practices for virtual team meetings include managing the meeting format, choreographing the meeting, and planning quality.

- **Meeting Format:** Working agreements and meeting protocols are formal in virtual teams to best manage the live time that team members spend together live. As indicated, meetings involve a short time for teambuilding to encourage trust and cohesion while most of the meeting time is spent discussing mutual issues, sharing data, and making decisions. Varying the time and medium of the meetings allows team members to stay engaged while not putting an undue burden on any team members in certain time zones. Project leaders re-emphasize the project purpose and team's mission at each and every meeting. Thus, *meeting format* includes the type of meeting, medium of the interaction, and the content.

- **Rigorous Planning:** While co-located teams can gather on short notice to discuss project tasks, virtual team meetings require *rigorous planning*. Team members gather infrequently so the time spent together must be value-added. It is important for the project leader to provide an agenda well in advance of the meeting, especially when team members have different native languages than the primary language selected for the project. Meeting minutes and follow-up assignments are discussed at the meeting and the project leader distributes written notes immediately after the meeting concludes. Software tools, especially those used for sharing information and team communications, are introduced during the project kick-off and not changed throughout the project to minimize distractions from the project's technical goals.

- **Quality Standards:** *Quality standards* for a project are clarified by the project charter. Team metrics include performance measures for team activities that surpass individual contributions. Key performance indicators (KPIs) for the technical, market, process, and team success are determined – with input from all virtual team members – during the project initiation and scoping phases. An *issues log* and discussion forums are maintained on shared drives so team members from all locations can measure progress toward the end goal.

**Q32: What does *Knowledge Management* mean for virtual teams?**

A32: All teams depend on gathering and analyzing data to make decisions. Information comes from a variety of stakeholders including key requirements for innovation projects from customers and sponsors. Features and functionalities are tracked as part of the product development effort throughout the project. Learning from lean product development, knowledge transfer and reuse are critical to accelerating innovation work. Systems engineering offers excellent traceability for product development, and there are dozens of internet and cloud options to increase collaboration for dispersed teams. While many project teams overlook lessons learned or post-launch reviews, it is important to gather these perspectives for continuous improvement of virtual teams.

- **Systems Engineering**: *Systems engineering* was discussed in Chapter 3 as a robust methodology for new product development. The key benefit of systems engineering for dispersed teams is traceability of work through version control. Each team member is always aware of the progress on each piece of the work and knows who has worked each portion of the project milestones and deliverables in the past. While the level of documentation for systems engineering may be excessive for face-to-face teams, it offers a vehicle for collaboration for dispersed team members. Since work assignments are often more technical in nature for virtual teams, systems engineering tools help to ensure accuracy and quality for technology development.

- **Collaboration Tools**: There are endless options for *collaboration* today using the internet and cloud filing systems. Most virtual team members access project information anywhere, anytime, and with any device. Webinars and meetings using video allow dispersed team members to see one another and for the project manager to ensure engagement during a meeting. Most live meeting software includes sharing tools, such as whiteboards and chat boxes. These options enhance virtual team communications. However, to minimize disruption for the project work, all team members are trained on the project software and sharing tools at the project kick-off and tools are not changed throughout the life of the project. If new software, cloud sharing, or virtual meeting tools are introduced, the project leader ensures that all team members have the bandwidth to use the new tools and full training is conducted. It is important to ensure ease-of-use for tools in a virtual team environment since remote team members often do not have equal access to IT support.

- **Lessons Learned**: The agile practice of frequent retrospectives is a benefit to virtual teams. Typically, if *lessons learned* are collected, it is at the end of a project. Virtual teams need to transfer knowledge and information throughout the life of the project to ensure proper interfaces and integration of the innovation work. Formal organizational practices support knowledge transfer and the project leader introduces opportunities during meetings to facilitate tacit knowledge transfer among the dispersed team members. In addition to discussing lessons learned during live meetings, discussion forums and shared databases are utilized for knowledge transfer among virtual team members.

**Q33:  How is *Leadership* different for virtual teams?**

A33:  Most literature available discusses leadership skills for face-to-face teams.  However, virtual teams require special skills for effective product development.  Virtual teams are more egalitarian, and leaders are more task oriented.  Directive or command-and-control leadership styles are usually ineffective for virtual teams due to the autonomous nature of the work and the strength of self-motivation among the team members.  Successful project leaders have an adaptive style, helping the dispersed team members build trust by clearly describing the project goals, setting expectations, and validating rigorous meeting protocols.  Site visits are important for both the project leader and team members.  Listening skills are a key to successful leadership in all situations but especially for engaging dispersed project team members.

- **Task-Oriented Leadership:**  Dispersed team members are selected for project participation based partly on their capacity for individual leadership skills and to represent local markets.  Motivation is less of an issue than in traditional teams, so the project manager has a different strategic and tactical role.  Reporting authority and project completion responsibility lie with the project leader.  Project status reports of scope completion, schedule, and budget are important for the project leader to emphasize, coordinate, and report to senior management.  The project leader works on administrative tasks to ensure team meetings, tools, and interactions are effective.  *Task-oriented leadership* is more tactical than for face-to-face innovation teams yet requires a greater degree of diplomacy for managing virtual team members.
- **Site Visits:**  One of the benefits of virtual teams is cost savings.  Some travel budget must be included in projects for the team leader to visit individual team members at their local sites as well as for *paired site visits*.  A paired site visit occurs when two team members meet at one site to conduct specific project tasks or activities.  Sometimes this occurs during supplier validation or equipment testing.  In other cases, individual

team members are brought together to write code, conduct quality audits, or complete other project activities. *Site visits* allow the project leader and the individual team members to build emotional trust as well as to interact with different potential customers, thus improving the overall innovation effort.

- **80/20 Listening:** Virtual team leaders have different roles, responsibilities, and tools to manage innovation teams. Leaders take a less directive approach and practice active listening with 80% of communication gathering data from team members and 20% talking or pushing information. Active listening is especially important for team members with second language skills so that the communication is clear, and decisions represent the consensus of the team. Repeating what was said, providing feedback, and questioning are characteristics of *80/20 listening*. Leaders of both virtual and face-to-face teams benefit from 80/20 listening.

### Q34: How is the VTM applied?

A34: When a new innovation team is formed with dispersed team members, the Virtual Team Model starts with *Initiation and Structure*. This element ensures that individual team members share the project vision through *Hiring for Purpose*. Newly formed teams also work through the *Communication* processes and establish ground rules for *Knowledge Management*.

Intact teams that are struggling to achieve innovation results enter the Virtual Team Model with the element and practices most important to closing communication gaps quickly. For instance, a dispersed team challenged with incomplete documentation and poor interfaces starts with the *Systems Engineering* practice. A team with missed deadlines and milestones enters the VTM with the *Meetings and Protocols* element to establish acceptable practices and procedures. In all cases, setting expectations for team behaviors in a virtual setting is critical to successful communication and achievement of innovation results.

More information on the Virtual Team Model (VTM), including team training opportunities, can be found at www.globalnpsolutions.com/vtm/. With appropriate training and implementation of the Virtual Team Model, new product development with dispersed teams can exceed the performance of co-located teams in meeting market needs, customer satisfaction, and time-to-commercialization.

## SUSTAINING GROWTH

**Q35: How do innovation leaders validate their experience?**

A35: Success in innovation requires continuous learning. Innovation leaders and NPD team members engage in training within their organizations to maintain knowledge of evolving processes, procedures, and policies. They also seek external training opportunities to build knowledge of technologies, markets, and trends. Certification programs demonstrate mastery of innovation information and expertise. Some preferred certification programs are briefly described. Each program requires continuing education to maintain certification, a hallmark of a strong leadership program.

- **NPDP:** New Product Development Professional (NPDP) certification is offered by the Product Development and Management Association (PDMA). The certification requires demonstration of knowledge by examination and years of experience practicing new product development.
- **PMP®:** Project Management Professionals (PMP®) demonstrate practical experience in managing projects and knowledge of the field by passing a certification exam. PMP certification is administered by the Project Management Institute (PMI®) and is globally recognized. Additional certifications are available from PMI for Agile Certified Practitioner (PMP-ACP®) or Portfolio Management Professional (PfMP®).
- **CPEM™:** The American Society of Engineering Managers (ASEM) administers the Certified Professional Engineering

Manager (CPEM) program. CPEM recognizes experienced professionals with technical and business knowledge who demonstrate industry and educational leadership.

More information on innovation, team, and leadership certification is available at www.Simple-PDH.com.

### Q36: How do innovation leaders sustain personal and professional growth?

A36: In addition to gaining and maintaining certification to demonstrate mastery of knowledge and practical experience, innovation leaders formally and informally sustain growth through mentoring, master mind groups, and coaching. Sharing challenges and solutions with people of similar backgrounds accelerates learning and professional growth. Innovation leaders that mentor and teach team members also grow by clarifying their thoughts, developing stronger analytical skills, and acquiring new knowledge.

### Q37: What is mentoring?

A37: Mentoring is a mutually beneficial relationship between two people seeking personal and professional growth. The *mentor* is usually more experienced, and the *mentee* is less experienced; nonetheless, both parties learn and grow from the relationship. Mentees learn technical skills and hope to advance their careers.

While the benefits to the mentee are obvious, mentors benefit from the relationship too. Mentors build leadership skills, improve their communication, and learn new perspectives. Most people find that serving as a mentor gives them great personal satisfaction as well. The relationship offers an opportunity to transfer tacit knowledge between generations of workers.

Many organizations have established formal mentoring programs, assigning managers and newer employees to mentor-mentee relationships. Formal mentoring helps build skills yet typically places responsibility for maintaining the relationship on the mentee. Sharing knowledge and information usually occurs during regularly scheduled meetings. Informal mentoring often takes place in organizations when a junior employee seeks the advice or feedback of a senior staff member. In either case, mutual trust and respect are necessary for successful mentoring relationships.

**Q38: What is a master mind group?**

A38: *Master mind groups* are a great way to sustain innovation learning, development, and growth. A master mind group has members of similar experience who serve in peer advisory roles for one another. The master mind group is typically facilitated by an expert who administers and manages the group including private discussion forums, documentation, and learning programs. Each group member benefits by *providing* help to others and *receiving* help from others in the group.

Master mind groups meet regularly, online or in-person. A typical meeting starts with celebration of goals met by group members, followed by open brainstorming sessions, and closing with established objectives for the next session. In this way, a master mind group drives accountability for action.

Each master mind group member participates in the open brainstorming session. Depending on the length and frequency of the meetings, each member puts forth a current challenge and other members advise potential solutions based upon their own experiences and knowledge. The facilitator may schedule educational sessions or guest speakers to address specific or recurring issues faced by the master mind group members. Often membership in a master mind group includes access to other information sources. For example, the **Innovation Master Mind** group from Global NP Solutions[1] includes access to the NPDP self-study course so that innovation leaders continue to build their knowledge base.

---

[1] For more information, please see https://globalnpsolutions.com/innovation-mastermind-imm/.

### Q39: How can innovation leaders benefit from coaching?

A39: *Coaching* involves personalized exploration by an innovation leader to improve skills and performance. Benefits of innovation coaching include accountability, enhanced emotional intelligence, improved motivation, and a more flexible leadership perspective. While mentoring primarily focuses on the development of technical skills for a junior employee, coaching focuses on growing leadership capacity for an experience new product practitioner or executive. Coaching is a more personal journey and emphasizes a "whole person" viewpoint, meaning that a leader must be effective across professional, social, family, and spiritual arenas to succeed in business and innovation. Coaching is not therapy and focuses on improving future performance.

Professional, executive, or innovation coaching is facilitated by a trained expert working closely with the innovation leader. Leaders identify their strengths and opportunities for improvement, including feedback from team members, fellow executives, customers, and direct reports. The coach observes the innovation leader in various work situations and provides tasks, activities, and advice to improve performance. Understanding leadership theory, motivators and stressors, and building self-awareness drive sustained improvements in innovation leadership and executive performance.

Innovation coaches have experience in new product development as well as leadership performance. When selecting an innovation coach, the leader is assured confidentiality, clarity of the coaching process, and demonstrated success in innovation and new product development. Innovation leaders typically work with a coach for a minimum of six months so that performance changes are realized. Many executives maintain a coaching relationship for years to provide continuous feedback and performance improvement as they advance through their careers.

**Q40: How does an innovation leader choose between a master mind group or innovation coaching?**

A40: All people are different and at different stages in their careers. Organizations have different cultures and maturity levels for product and process development. Innovation leaders achieve accountability through both master mind groups and coaching. Joining a master mind group includes a commitment to share experiences and knowledge to build the capabilities of the leader and of other group members quickly. Master mind group members openly share their challenges and growth opportunities. They must be willing to both give and receive help and to actively participate in each meeting.

Innovation coaching is personal and in-depth to address performance improvements. Coaching touches all areas of a leader's life, including their worries about family as well as business challenges. Introspection and a willingness to test new behaviors is critical to successful coaching engagements. Many people start a journey to enhancing their innovation skills through a master mind group and then migrate to individual coaching relationships. However, many executives that are stretched for time engage in innovation coaching initially so they can implement rapid improvements in their organization and quickly demonstrate new product development success. Peer coaching is also appropriate for new and intact innovation teams to improve team management skills and realize higher quality results.

## INNOVATION TRAPS FOR A SUSTAINING ORGANIZATION

- ➢ Using a single metric to gauge innovation success.
- ➢ Allowing metrics to serve as a surrogate for strategy and compensating for achieving metrics rather than innovation goals.
- ➢ Lack of clarity of innovation management and executive leadership roles and responsibilities.
- ➢ Not following the Virtual Team Model (VTM) to execute new product development with a dispersed team.
- ➢ Failing to continuously learn and grow through a master mind group or innovation coaching.

# CHAPTER 6

## THE INNOVATION CODE OF CONDUCT

*They spend their years in prosperity and go down to the grave in peace.*
*Job 21:13 (NIV)*

**Q1:  What is a code of conduct?**

A1:  A *code of conduct* is a set of principles, rules, operating conditions, and responsibilities expected of the members of a group.  Individual behaviors should align with the code of conduct to maintain professionalism within the organization.  Formal trade associations usually document their code of conduct to maintain professional standards and behaviors for their members.

**Q2:  How is a code of conduct different than ethics?**

A2:  *Ethics* reflect the values and morals of an organization or societal group.  A code of ethics frames the regulations of a group describing moral expectations and violations of the value systems.  A code of ethics guides decisions and indicates values and morals that are acceptable to individuals and to the group.  Decisions are guided by ethics while behaviors reflect the code of conduct. In short, the ethical standards of an organization describe what is right and what is wrong from the group's fundamental value perspective.

**Q3:  What are common ethical theories?**

A3:  Ethical standards are based on underlying domains of decision-making models to support a system of rules or principles.  Theories of ethics inform decisions.  Some ethical conduct theories follow [1].

- **Teleological Theory:**  Also known as *ethical egoism*, the *teleological theory* of ethics asserts that the consequences of actions determine whether those actions were right or wrong. The rightness of an act is demonstrated by the result.

- **Utilitarian Theory:**  The *utilitarian theories* of ethics focus on maximizing good.  "Utility" has many different definitions in this context, but the best action is the one that maximizes utility.
- **Altruistic Theory:**  Moral actions that show concern for others is called *altruistic ethical theory*.  Altruism means acting in the best interest of others rather than in one's own self-interest.
- **Virtue-Based Theory:**  In contrast to setting rules, the *virtue-based theory* of ethics focuses on a leader's character.  When individuals develop good character traits, like kindness and generosity, they can make correct decisions later in life.

### Q4:  What are the fundamental ethical principles for an innovation leader?

A4:  Fundamentally, innovation leaders act within ethical standards that drive their conduct to be honest, fair, respectful, and responsible. The ethical principles for *Flagship Innovation Leaders* are built from those of the American Society of Engineering Management (ASEM) and the Project Management Institute (PMI®).

- **Honesty and Fairness:**  Being honest and fair in serving internal and external stakeholders throughout the innovation ecosystem is a key tenet of ethical leadership.  Professional conduct is bound by a duty of fairness to make decisions and act impartially and objectively.   Honesty and fairness are demonstrated by conduct of innovation leaders that is free from competing self-interest, prejudice, or favoritism. Innovation leaders demonstrate transparency in the decision-making process and provide equal access to information for all who are authorized to have that information.  Contracts are not awarded that provide personal gain at the expense of others. Hiring practices do not discriminate against others based on gender, gender identity, race, religion, age, disability, nationality, or sexual orientation. When a conflict of interest arises, an innovation leader invokes the principles of honesty and fairness to refrain from engaging in the decision-making process or in other matters of influence.

- **Respect:** Innovation leaders are respectful of other peoples' values and decisions, showing empathy, and being tolerant of opposing viewpoints. Respectful innovation leaders have a duty to show a high regard for themselves, others, and the resources entrusted to them. Innovation practitioners inform themselves of the norms and customs of others and avoid engaging in behaviors that might be perceived as disrespectful. Negotiations are always in good faith and property rights of others are respected in full.

- **Responsibility:** Responsibility is the duty of an innovation leader to take ownership for decisions that are made or omitted, for actions that are taken or that fail to be taken, and consequences of any actions taken. Innovation leaders and new product development practitioners have a commitment to public safety, health, and the environment. Innovation leaders strive to increase their competency and the professionalism within the practices and standards of innovation. It is the responsibility of innovation leaders to use their knowledge and skill to fulfill commitments, to acknowledge and correct errors or omissions promptly, and to protect confidential information as necessary and as required by the law.

**Q5: What is the code of conduct for an innovation leader?**

A5: Innovation leaders act with honesty, fairness, respect, and responsibility. Behaviors that reflect the code of ethics include the following.

- Hold paramount the safety, health, and welfare of the public and the environment.

- Protect and hold confidential the private and identifying information of customers, clients, and potential customers unless explicitly authorized otherwise.
- Maintain professional competencies, certifications, and licenses to advance innovation and to practice as a professional innovation leader.
- Give proper credit for the work of others and accept and give professional criticism.
- Abide by the laws, regulations, and policies of nations, states, and communities where innovations are developed or deployed.
- Act in a professional and ethical manner to all internal and external stakeholders.

APPENDIX

Global NP Solutions, LLC
tereta@globalnpsolutions.com
info@Simple-PDH.com

**INNOVATION HEALTH ASSESSMENT REPORT**

*Your Company* Results

**Prepared for:**   Example (example@mail.com)                    **Date:** DD-MM-YYYY

The *Innovation Health Assessment* is a benchmarking survey designed for chief technology officers, innovation professionals, new product development practitioners, and R&D teams to assess the maturity of their innovation ecosystem. A brief summary of *Your Company*'s innovation health follows, compared to all-industry average (light shading in the figure).

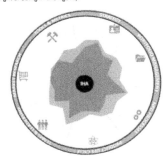

*Your Company* demonstrates some strength in **strategic alignment** but, like many organizations, demonstrates weakness in resource allocation. In comparison to all-industry averages, *Your Company* tries to ensure every new product development project is driven by at least one strategic objective. However, as a result of poor resource allocation, innovation projects are more costly and result in delayed market launches. We recommend streamlining the strategy through a *Strategy Alignment Workshop*. Additionally, since strategy design and development are senior leadership tasks, managers involved in product development programs can benefit from collaboration and problem-solving through an *Innovation Master Mind Group*. Weakness in project alignment with growth objectives can be remedied through identification of more creative product, technology, and market opportunities. Learning through an *Intensive Design Thinking Workshop* and *Disruptive and Open Innovation* helps organizations to generate more creative alternatives to meet strategic goals.

**Product Portfolio Management** (PPM) is frequently an area of underperformance for many firms. Companies that align innovation project selection and investment with strategic goals outperform their competitors by significant margins. As indicated, PPM is an area of weakness for organizations across all industries, but *Your Company* shows particular weakness in regularly reviewing innovation projects for value and fit with strategy. There are opportunities to improve comparative

www.globalnpsolutions.com
www.simple-pdh.com
+1 (281) 787-3979
page 1

175

Global NP Solutions, LLC
teresa@globalnpsolutions.com
info@Simple-PDH.com

evaluations of innovation projects competing for the same resources and *Your Company* can benefit from instituting *Product Portfolio Management in 100 Days*. This program includes a deep dive examination of *Your Company's* strategy, decision-making, and project selection tools resulting in a streamlined portfolio of new product development projects that are adequately resourced to meet short-term and long-range objectives. Further, *Your Company* can improve project selection and delivery through *Six Sigma and NPD Tools* training as well as building better team relationships for effective decision-making through *The Five Behaviors of a Cohesive Team®*.

Firms that follow established **New Product Development (NPD) Processes**, whether traditional or Agile systems, succeed in innovation by quickly advancing the most valuable projects. Industry-wide averages demonstrate well-documented processes and training for all innovation team members. NPD processes are reviewed regularly among highest performers to adopt emerging practices and ensure efficient new product design that is linked to customer needs. *Innovation Best Practices Workshop* allows *Your Company* to identify gaps with industry-wide best practices in new product process design and project implementation. Decision-making by gatekeepers and project sponsors is improved along with the quality of ideas entering the innovation process when teams are familiar with *Product Development Fundamentals* and can manage projects with the tools and techniques from a *Project Management Bootcamp* (emphasizing project delivery, schedule, budget, and risk management). *Your Company* can also benefit from an *Agile NPD Workshop* in order to improve customer feedback during projects and *Everything DiSC® Management* to enhance understanding of individual work styles for innovation teams working on high-risk technology developments.

Since *Your Company* operates within the *Consumer-Packaged Goods* industry, you demonstrate stability with the **Product Life Cycle** but have opportunities for improvement compared to the all-industry benchmark. You may wish to consider training in *The Product Life Cycle* when on-boarding new team members and as a refresher for intact product development teams. Pricing strategies and product life cycle are also discussed in *Innovation Best Practices Workshop*. Innovation teams also benefit from *Team Dimensions Group Profile* to understand roles through the life of a product development effort and linking development cycles to individual work styles. *Managing Scientists, Engineers, and Designers* helps technically trained team members to better understand customer needs, product life cycles, and *The Business of Product Management*.

Your Company shows distinct weaknesses in **Teams and Leadership** in executing new product development projects, especially in incorporating customer feedback for successful product design. We recommend several remedies, including *Product Development Fundamentals, Intensive Design Thinking Workshop, Innovation Best Practices Workshop, Everything DiSC® Management, Situational Leadership®,* and *Five Behaviors of a Cohesive Team™* training to help build productive teams with appropriate decision-making authority. *Your Company* may also wish to enhance training for engineering managers through *Managing Scientists, Engineers, and Designers*. An important aspect of innovation leadership is *Changing the Culture for Innovation Success* since failure, risk, and success metrics are radically different for innovation work than in standard operational functions. Senior executives benefit from *Innovation Master Mind* and *Gold Level Leadership Coaching* to share ideas, challenges, and practical knowledge with like-minded innovation leaders across an industry-wide spectrum. These personalized growth programs speed time of implementation and directly yield enhanced innovation ecosystem improvements.

www.globalnpsolutions.com
www.simple-pdh.com
+1 (281) 787-3979
page 2

Global NP Solutions, LLC
teresa@globalnpsolutions.com
info@Simple-PDH.com

Generally, *Your Company* is performing effectively in **Market Research**, most likely associated with the markets for *Consumer-Packaged Goods*. While many companies have room for improvement in bridging customer insights to selecting ideas for product development, *Your Company* compares favorably to the all-industry average. To gain a competitive advantage, *Your Company* can optimize customer insights through improved metrics design and ideation tools. These topics are addressed through *Product Development Fundamentals, Design Thinking Workshops, Strategy Alignment Workshop,* and *Market Study and Resource Workshop.* Market research is the most commonly overlooked factor in successful new product development, including executive decisions to retire products that are no longer profitable. Decision-making can be improved through *The Business of Product Management* and *PPM in 100 Days.* Innovation leaders sustain innovation success through dialogue with other experienced innovation professionals in the *Innovation Master Mind.*

*Your Company* generally compares well against industry averages but shows some areas for improvement in deploying **Innovation Tools and Metrics.** Many firms use lagging metrics to measure progress in new product development, but only leading metrics yield change in team and project performance. To learn more about which tools and metrics to use in your innovation programs, *Your Company* can benefit from *NPD Best Practices Workshop, Project Management Bootcamp,* and *Six Sigma and NPD Tools.* Tools and metrics must support the organization's innovation processes and provide strategic alignment. *PPM in 100 Days* helps organizations identify leading metrics and teaches innovation leaders how to select the highest value projects for execution.

## Summary

*Your Company* is well positioned to grow and prosper from innovation. Results from your **Innovation Health Assessment** indicated an overall score of *61.8 points* (based on an average of data inputs from three participants). This indicates an organization that is *Adopting* an innovation ecosystem and designing policies, practices, and procedures that will benefit new product development over the long-term. *Your Company* is on the cusp of *Transforming* into a mature innovation organization that can lead in the *Consumer-Packaged Goods* industry.

Your innovation team has an average of *10 years* of experience in the field of innovation, working in roles of *R&D Director, Program Manager,* and *Project Lead.* As you consider career pathways for innovation leaders at *Your Company,* your teams will demonstrate mastery of innovation, project management, and leadership skills with *New Product Development Professional (NPDP)* certification and the *Project Management Professional (PMP®)* credential. Both of these certifications benefit individuals in advancing their career internally or with new organizational structures. The *Certified Professional Engineering Manager (CPEM®)* is another credential offered for team members to demonstrate competency and capacity as they transition from technical to leadership roles in new product development.

Our goal at *Global NP Solutions* and **Simple-PDH** is to *Build Innovation Leaders.* Please feel free to contact me with further questions or comments about *Your Company's* **Innovation Health Assessment** and opportunities to take your innovation ecosystem to the next level!

Global NP Solutions, LLC
teresa@globalnpsolutions.com
info@Simple-PDH.com

## FLAGSHIP INNOVATION LEADER

Without clearly defined innovation processes, new products fail at unusually high rates. Let us help you design and negotiate an effective and efficient innovation ecosystem that allows you to improve time-to-market, increase customer satisfaction, develop leadership talent, and build productive innovation teams.

Our *Flagship Innovation Leader* program allows you to select the courses you need according to your organization's innovation maturity. We recommend starting with an *Innovation Health Assessment* to benchmark internal new product development practices against the most successful firms. To allow convenience for scheduling and adaptive learning, courses and workshops can be delivered at separate times or combined into consecutive, multi-day events.

We will customize the training materials to provide unique learning and application of the information so you can immediately implement innovation system enhancements. Training programs are facilitated online or onsite while workshops are held in a creative space to generate the best solutions for your innovation program. Many of the individual courses in the *Flagship Innovation Leader* curriculum offer external formal certification upon completion of the workshop with demonstration of knowledge and experience with the certifying body.

### LEARNING

- Product Development Fundamentals
- Disruptive and Open Innovation
- Intensive Design Thinking Workshop
- Team Dimensions Profile*

### ADOPTING

- Innovation Best Practices Workshop
  - NPDP Certification available through PDMA
- Everything DiSC® Management*
- Project Management Bootcamp
  - PMP® Certification available through PMI®
- Agile NPD Training and Workshop
- Situational Team Leadership®*
- Changing the Culture for Innovation Success
- Six Sigma and NPD Tools
- Managing Scientists, Engineers, and Designers
  - CPEM® Certification available through ASEM

### TRANSFORMING

- Five Behaviors of a Cohesive Team™*
- Scrum Master Training
  - SMC Certification available through SCRUMStudy™
- Strategy Alignment Workshop
- The Product Life Cycle
- Product Portfolio Management (PPM) in 100 Days
- Market Study and Resource Workshop
- Virtual Team (VTM) Training

### SUSTAINING

- Everything DiSC® Agile EQ*
- The Business of Product Management
- Sustaining Innovation Success
  - Innovation Master Mind
  - Gold Level Leadership Coaching

*Available through JHC Authorized Partner Network

www.globalnpsolutions.com
www.simple-pdh.com
+1 (281) 787-3979
page 4

178

# REFERENCES

## CHAPTER 1

1. W. Koetzier and A. Alon, "*Accenture: Why Low Risk Innovation is Costly*," 2013. [Online]. Available: http://www.innovacion.cl/wp-content/uploads/2013/05/Accenture-Why-Low-Risk-Innovation-Costly.pdf. [Accessed 27 March 2018].

## CHAPTER 2

1. H. Williams, "*Marketers Falling Behind Consumer Demand*," 24 August 2017. [Online]. Available: https://www.exchangewire.com/blog/2017/08/24/marketers-falling-behind-consumer-demand-innovation-instagram-rise-uk/. [Accessed 27 March 2018].
2. C. C. Markides, *All the Right Moves: A Guide to Crafting Breakthrough Strategy*, Boston, MA: Harvard Business Press Books, 1999.
3. R. G. Cooper, *Winning at New Products*, 5th ed., New York, NY: Basic Books, 2017.
4. R. E. Miles and C. C. Snow, *Organizational Strategy, Structure, and Process*, New York: McGraw-Hill, 1978.
5. A. Osterwalder and Y. Pigneur, *Business Model Generation*, Hoboken, NJ: Wiley, 2010.
6. M. Antonisse and P. Metz, "Sustainable Innovation," *Visions*, pp. 8-13, Quarter 2 2013.
7. H. Shah, Ed., *A Guide to the Engineering Management Body of Knowledge*, Rolla, MO: The American Society for Engineering Management, 2012.
8. C. M. Christensen, *The Innovator's Dilemma: When New Technologies Cause Great Firms to Fail*, Boston, MA: Harvard Business School Press, 1997.
9. H. W. Chesbrough, "The Era of Open Innovation," *MIT Sloan Management,* vol. 44, no. 3, pp. 35-41, Spring 2003.
10. B. W. Mattimore, *Idea Stormers: How to Lead and Inspire Creative Breakthroughs*, San Francisco, CA: Jossy-Bass, 2012.

## CHAPTER 3

1. H. Thota and M. Zunaira, *Key Concepts in Innovation*, New York: Palgrave Macmillan, 2011.
2. R. G. Cooper, *Winning at New Products*, 5th ed., New York, NY: Basic Books, 2017.
3. K. Eling and C. Herstatt, "Managing the Front End of Innovation - Less Fuzzy, Yet Still Not Fully Understood," *Journal of Product Innovation and Management,* vol. 34, no. 6, pp. 864-874, 2017.
4. Defense Acquisition University, *Systems Engineering Fundamentals*, Fort Belvoir, VA: US Department of Defense, 2001.
5. D. L. Goetch and S. B. Davis, *Quality Management for Organizational Excellence*, Boston: Pearson, 2016.
6. C. M. Rodriguez, *Product Design and Innovation*, Amazon Create Space, 2016.
7. "*Manifesto for Agile Software Development*," 2001. [Online]. Available: https://agilemanifesto.org/. [Accessed 19 July 2019].
8. R. G. Cooper, *Winning at New Products*, 5th ed., New York, NY: Basic Books, 2017.

9.    A. C. Ward and D. K. Sobek II, *Lean Product and Process Development*, 2nd ed., Cambridge, MA: Lean Enterprises Institute, Inc., 2014.
10.   R. Mascitelli, *Mastering Lean Product Development*, Northridge, CA: Technology Perspectives, 2011.
11.   E. Ries, *The Lean Startup*, New York: Crown Business, 2011.

## CHAPTER 4

1.    P. Kotler and K. L. Keller, *Marketing Management*, 12th ed. ed., Upper Saddle River, NJ: Pearson Prentice Hall, 2006.
2.    R. G. Cooper, S. J. Edgett and E. J. Kleinschmidt, *Portfolio Management for New Products*, 2nd ed. ed., New York: Basic Books, 2001.
3.    T. Jurgens-Kowal, *"Talking to Your Bo$$ - The Economics of Engineering,"* 19 October 2010. [Online]. Available: https://www.aiche.org/chenected/series/talking-your-bo-economics-engineering. [Accessed 28 August 2019].
4.    S. K. Markham and H. Lee, "Product Development and Management Association's 2012 Comparative Performance Assessment Study," *Journal of Product Innovation Management,* vol. 30, no. 3, pp. 408-429, 2013.
5.    B. W. Tuckman, "Devlopmental Sequence in Small Groups (reprint)," *Group Facilitation: A Research and Applications Journal,* pp. 66-81, Spring 2001.
6.    M. Scullard, PhD and D. Baum, Ed.D., *Everything DiSC® Manual*, Minneapolis, MN: Wiley, 2015.
7.    P. Lencioni, *The Five Dysfunctions of a Team*, San Francisco, CA: Jossey-Bass, 2002.
8.    R. B. Rosenfeld, G. J. Wilhelmi and A. Harrison, *The Invisible Element*, Idea Connection Systems, 2011.
9.    R. H. Kilman and K. W. Thomas, "Four Perspectives on Conflict Management: An Attributional Framework for Organizing Descriptive and Normative Theory," *The Academy of Management Review,* vol. 3, no. 1, pp. 59-68, January 1978.
10.   Inscape Publishing, *"Team Dimensions Profile 2.0,"* Inscape Publishing, Inc., 2006.
11.   S. C. Wheelwright and K. B. Clark, *Revolutionizing Product Development: Quantum Leaps in Speed, Efficiency, and Quality*, New York: The Free Press, 1992.
12.   C. M. Christensen, *The Innovator's Dilemma: When New Technologies Cause Great Firms to Fail*, Boston, MA: Harvard Business School Press, 1997.

## CHAPTER 5

1.    R. S. Kaplan and D. P. Norton, "Using the Balanced Scorecard as a Strategic Management System," *Harvard Business Review,* pp. 75-85, January-February 1996.
2.    M. Harris and B. Taylor, "Don't Let Metrics Undermine Your Business," *Harvard Business Review,* pp. 62-69, September-October 2019.
3.    J. Greenberg, *Managing Behavior in Organizations*, 5th ed., Boston: Prentice-Hall, 2010.
4.    R. W. Griffin, *Fundamentals of Management*, 7th ed., Mason, OH: South-Western (Cengage), 2014.
5.    D. Goleman, "What Makes a Leader?," *Harvard Business Review,* pp. 93-102, November-December 1998.
6.    T. A. Jurgens-Kowal, "Bridging Communication Gaps in Virtual Teams," in *Proceedings of the American Society of Engineering Management 2016 International Annual Conference*, Red Hook, NY, 2016.

7.   T. Jurgens-Kowal and D. Hardenbrook, "Bridging Communication Gaps in Virtual Teams," in *Leveraging Constraints for Innovation*, PDMA New Product Development Essentials, Volume 3, Hoboken, NJ: Wiley, 218, pp. 95-117.

## CHAPTER 6

1.   H. Shah, Ed., *A Guide to the Engineering Management Body of Knowledge*, Rolla, MO: The American Society for Engineering Management, 2012.

# ABOUT THE AUTHOR

**Teresa Jurgens-Kowal** is passionate about innovation. She is a writer, mentor, coach, and trainer. Teresa founded Global NP Solutions in 2009 to help individuals and organizations learn, adopt, transform, and sustain innovation. She enjoys helping people reach their highest levels of success with innovation. Teresa's consulting clients include a full spectrum of large industry corporations to entrepreneurs seeking to launch new products. She coaches executives and managers to improve innovation performance using a variety of work style assessments and customized tools. Teresa frequently presents keynotes and breakouts locally and nationally on her favorite topics of innovation, design thinking, and product development.

As a Registered Education Provider (REP) with the Product Development and Management Association (PDMA), Teresa has written the #1 best-selling book for New Product Development Professional (NPDP) certification, *NPDP Certification Exam Prep: A 24-Hour Study Guide*. She recently published a chapter on leading virtual teams for innovation projects with the *Virtual Team Model (VTM)* (October 2018, *Leveraging Constraints for Innovation*).

Prior to founding Global NP Solutions, Teresa worked in R&D, process technology development, and as an internal innovation expert at ExxonMobil Chemical Company. She has degrees in Chemical engineering from the University of Washington (PhD) and University of Idaho (BS), and an MBA from West Texas A&M University. Teresa lives in Southeast Texas and enjoys bicycling and scrapbooking.

**GLOBAL NP SOLUTIONS**
*Building Innovation Leaders*

Made in the USA
Monee, IL
15 April 2021